Math Achievement
Enriching Activities Based on NCTM Standards

Grade 5

by
**Gina Monteleone
and
Jennifer Moore**

Table of Contents

Introduction

Welcome to the **Math Achievement** series! Each book in this series is designed to reinforce the math skills appropriate for each grade level and to encourage high-level thinking and problem-solving skills. Enhancing students' thinking and problem-solving abilities can help them succeed in all academic areas. In addition, experiencing success in math can increase a student's confidence and self-esteem, both in and out of the classroom.

Each **Math Achievement** book offers challenging questions **based on the standards specified by the National Council of Teachers of Mathematics (NCTM)**. All five content standards (number and operations, algebra, geometry, measurement, data analysis and probability) and the process standard, problem solving, are covered in the activities.

The questions and format are similar to those found on standardized math tests. The experience students gain from answering questions in this format may help increase their test scores.

These exercises can be used to enhance the regular math curriculum, to individualize instruction, to provide extra practice for home schoolers, or to review skills between grades.

The following math skills are covered in this book:

- **problem solving**
- **place value**
- **estimation**
- **addition**
- **subtraction**
- **multiplication**
- **division**
- **fractions**
- **decimals**
- **ratio and percent**
- **calendar**
- **time**
- **money**
- **measurement**
- **geometry**
- **tables and graphs**
- **probability & statistics**

Each **Math Achievement** book contains **four pretests in standardized test format** at the beginning of each book. The pretests have been designed so that they may be used individually, as four stand-alone tests, or in groups. They may be used to identify students' needs in specific areas, or to compare students' math abilities at the beginning and end of the school year. **A scoring box is also included on each activity page.** This scoring box can be programmed to suit your specific classroom and student needs with total problems, total correct, and score.

Read each problem. Circle the letter beside the correct answer.

1. The standard form for four thousand, eight hundred thirty-nine is _____ .

   A. 4,893   B. 4,839   C. 400,809   D. 4,008,039

2. 9,000 + 800 + 50 + 1 is the expanded form of: A. 5,891   B. 90,851   C. 980,561   D. 9,851

3.   785
        + 17

   A. 792
   B. 802
   C. 812
   D. 822

6.   6,192
        + 5,289

   A. 12,121
   B. 13,471
   C. 11,841
   D. 11,481

9.   2,809
        8,315
        + 6,492

   A. 17,616
   B. 17,805
   C. 18,739
   D. 16,093

4.   6,182
        − 1,392

   A. 5,221
   B. 7,212
   C. 4,790
   D. 5,791

7.   62,450
        − 8,025

   A. 70,475
   B. 54,425
   C. 60,392
   D. 82,759

10.   3,987
        x   8

   A. 24,782
   B. 32,981
   C. 31,896
   D. 39,287

5. $9.39
        x   23

   A. $228.47
   B. $288.26
   C. $183.89
   D. $215.97

8. $30 \overline{)196}$

   A. 5 R26
   B. 6 R16
   C. 6 R22
   D. 7 R2

11. $45 \overline{)1,094}$

   A. 22 R19
   B. 24 R33
   C. 24 R14
   D. 20 R39

12. How many buses are needed to carry 320 students on a school trip if each bus can carry 80 students?

   A. 4 buses   B. 6 buses   C. 3 buses   D. 2 buses

4

Total Problems: _____   Total Correct: _____   Score: _____

Read each problem. Circle the letter beside the correct answer.

1. Malcolm collected $222.40 from his paper route. He delivers to 32 families. How much does each family pay?

    A. $6.95
    B. $7.25
    C. $7.85
    D. $6.99

---

2. Which of the following is **not** true about a right angle?

    A. It has 2 rays with a common endpoint.
    B. It measures 90⁰.
    C. It has three equal sides.

3. Which figure is an octagon?

    A.   B. 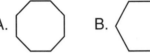   C.

---

4. Which figure is a right angle?

    A.    B.   C.

5. Which is true about a triangle?

    A. It has 3 sides and 3 vertices.
    B. It has 4 sides and 4 vertices.
    C. It must have 1 right angle.
    D. It has 5 sides and 5 vertices.

---

6. A quadrilateral with all sides the same length is a _____ .

    A. rectangle   C. square
    B. triangle   D. hexagon

7. Which figure is an obtuse angle?

    A.   B.   C.

---

8. The distance through the center of a circle is _____ .

    A. the radius   B. the ulna   C. the diameter   D. the endpoint

---

9. James is building a sandbox at the local elementary school. He wants the sandbox to measure 8 feet on each side. How many feet of wood does he need to buy for the frame?

    A. 40 feet   B. 30 feet   C. 32 feet   D. 16 feet

Total Problems:	Total Correct:	Score:

Read each problem. Circle the letter beside the correct answer.

1. How would $6\frac{9}{10}$ be written as a decimal?

    A. 9.6   B. 6.09   C. 6.9   D. 6.10

2. The correct decimal form for $8\frac{7}{10}$ is _____ .

    A. 8.07   B. 8.7   C. 7.8   D. 7.08

3. The fraction $\frac{35}{100}$ is written as the decimal .35, and is read "thirty-five-hundredths." How
    would $\frac{28}{100}$ be written as a decimal?

    A. .35   B. 28.00   C. .028   D. .28

4. What is the correct decimal form for fifty-two-hundredths?

    A. .52   B. .052   C. 52.00   D. 5.20

5. $\begin{array}{r} .8 \\ + .3 \\ \hline \end{array}$ A. .11
                                                            B. 1.1
                                                            C. .5

6. $\begin{array}{r} .4 \\ + .5 \\ \hline \end{array}$ A. .1
                                                            B. .9
                                                            C. .7

7. $\begin{array}{r} .731 \\ + .145 \\ \hline \end{array}$ A. .0814
                                                               B. 8.76
                                                               C. .876

8. Jordan ran the 100-meter dash in 11.07 seconds. Richard ran it in 12.12 seconds, and
    Scott ran it in 11.19 seconds. Who came in first place?

    A. Jordan   B. Richard   C. Scott

9. Carl won the pole vault event with a jump of 5.35 meters. Charles placed second with a
    vault of 4.75 meters. How much higher did Carl vault than Charles?

    A. 1.4 meters   B. .75 meters   C. .6 meters

10. During one rainstorm, 1.13 inches of rain fell. During a second storm, 2.31 inches of rain
    fell. Altogether, how much rain fell during the two storms?

    A. 3.44 inches   B. 1.09 inches   C. 2.34 inches

11. If there are 12 girls and 17 boys in the fifth grade class, what is the ratio of girls to boys?

    A. $\frac{1}{2}$ B. $\frac{17}{12}$ C. $\frac{12}{17}$ D. $\frac{12}{2}$

6

| Total Problems: | Total Correct: | Score: |

The chart shows student absences from school for one month. Use the chart to solve the following problems. Circle the letter beside the correct answer.

Student Absences for One Month

	Monday	Tuesday	Wednesday	Thursday	Friday
Week 1	13	23	21	15	16
Week 2	12	10	16	22	24
Week 3	28	11	14	14	10
Week 4	20	19	16	17	12

1. What was the average number of absences during Week 1? Show your work.

   A. 23   C. 19.2

   B. 20.5   D. 17.6

3. What was the range of absences for the month? Show your work.

   A. 10   C. 18

   B. 20   D. 23

2. What was the average number of absences on Fridays during this month? Show your work.

   A. 15.5   C. 27.1

   B. 14.8   D. 16

4. Which day had the highest average number of absences? Show your work.

   A. Monday   C. Thursday

   B. Tuesday   D. Friday

Total Problems: _____   Total Correct: _____   Score: _____

Page 4

Name _____ Pretest

Read each problem. Circle the letter beside the correct answer.

1. The standard form for four thousand, eight hundred thirty-nine is _____.

   A. 4,893   (B.) 4,839   C. 400,809   D. 4,008,039

2. 9,000 + 800 + 50 + 1 is the expanded form of: A. 5,891   B. 90,851   C. 980,561   (D.) 9,851

3. 785
   + 17

   A. 792
   (B.) 802
   C. 812
   D. 822

6. 6,192
   + 5,289

   A. 12,121
   B. 13,471
   C. 11,841
   (D.) 11,481

9. 2,809
   8,315
   + 6,492

   (A.) 17,616
   B. 17,805
   C. 18,739
   D. 16,093

4. 6,182
   − 1,392

   A. 5,221
   B. 7,212
   (C.) 4,790
   D. 5,791

7. 62,450
   − 8,025

   A. 70,475
   (B.) 54,425
   C. 60,392
   D. 82,759

10. 3,987
    x   8

    A. 24,782
    B. 32,981
    (C.) 31,896
    D. 39,287

5. $9.39
   x 23

   A. $228.47
   B. $288.26
   C. $183.89
   (D.) $215.97

8. 30 | 196

   A. 5 R26
   (B.) 6 R16
   C. 6 R22
   D. 7 R2

11. 45 | 1,094

    A. 22 R19
    B. 24 R33
    (C.) 24 R14
    D. 20 R39

12. How many buses are needed to carry 320 students on a school trip if each bus can carry 80 students?

    (A.) 4 buses   B. 6 buses   C. 3 buses   D. 2 buses

4 | Total Problems: ____ Total Correct: ____ Score: ____ | © Carson-Dellosa CD-2212

Page 5

Name _____ Pretest

Read each problem. Circle the letter beside the correct answer.

1. Malcolm collected $222.40 from his paper route. He delivers to 32 families. How much does each family pay?

   (A.) $6.95
   B. $7.25
   C. $7.85
   D. $6.99

2. Which of the following is **not** true about a right angle?

   A. It has 2 rays with a common endpoint.
   B. It measures 90°.
   (C.) It has three equal sides.

3. Which figure is an octagon?

   (A.) ⬡   B. ⬡   C. ▢

4. Which figure is a right angle?

   A.   (B.)   C.

5. Which is true about a triangle?

   (A.) It has 3 sides and 3 vertices.
   B. It has 4 sides and 4 vertices.
   C. It must have 1 right angle.
   D. It has 5 sides and 5 vertices.

6. A quadrilateral with all sides the same length is a _____.

   A. rectangle   (C.) square
   B. triangle   D. hexagon

7. Which figure is an obtuse angle?

   A.   (B.)   C.

8. The distance through the center of a circle is _____.

   A. the radius   B. the ulna   (C.) the diameter   D. the endpoint

9. James is building a sandbox at the local elementary school. He wants the sandbox to measure 8 feet on each side. How many feet of wood does he need to buy for the frame?

   A. 40 feet   B. 30 feet   (C.) 32 feet   D. 16 feet

© Carson-Dellosa CD-2212 | Total Problems: ____ Total Correct: ____ Score: ____ | **5**

Page 6

Name _____ Pretest

Read each problem. Circle the letter beside the correct answer.

1. How would $6\frac{9}{10}$ be written as a decimal?

   A. 9.6   B. 6.09   (C.) 6.9   D. 6.10

2. The correct decimal form for $8\frac{7}{10}$ is _____.

   A. 8.07   (B.) 8.7   C. 7.8   D. 7.08

3. The fraction $\frac{35}{100}$ is written as the decimal .35, and is read "thirty-five-hundredths." How would $\frac{28}{100}$ be written as a decimal?

   A. .35   B. 28.00   C. .028   (D.) .28

4. What is the correct decimal form for fifty-two-hundredths?

   (A.) .52   B. .052   C. 52.00   D. 5.20

5. .8
   + .3

   A. .11
   (B.) 1.1
   C. .5

6. .4
   + .5

   A. .1
   (B.) .9
   C. .7

7. .731
   + .145

   A. .0814
   B. 8.76
   (C.) .876

8. Jordan ran the 100-meter dash in 11.07 seconds. Richard ran it in 12.12 seconds, and Scott ran it in 11.19 seconds. Who came in first place?

   (A.) Jordan   B. Richard   C. Scott

9. Carl won the pole vault event with a jump of 5.35 meters. Charles placed second with a vault of 4.75 meters. How much higher did Carl vault than Charles?

   A. 1.4 meters   B. .75 meters   (C.) .6 meters

10. During one rainstorm, 1.13 inches of rain fell. During a second storm, 2.31 inches of rain fell. Altogether, how much rain fell during the two storms?

    (A.) 3.44 inches   B. 1.09 inches   C. 2.34 inches

11. If there are 12 girls and 17 boys in the fifth grade class, what is the ratio of girls to boys?

    A. $\frac{1}{2}$ B. $\frac{17}{12}$ (C.) $\frac{12}{17}$ D. $\frac{12}{2}$

6 | Total Problems: ____ Total Correct: ____ Score: ____ | © Carson-Dellosa CD-2212

Page 7

Name _____ Pretest

The chart shows student absences from school for one month. Use the chart to solve the following problems. Circle the letter beside the correct answer.

Student Absences for One Month

	Monday	Tuesday	Wednesday	Thursday	Friday
Week 1	13	23	21	15	16
Week 2	12	10	16	22	24
Week 3	28	11	14	14	10
Week 4	20	19	16	17	12

1. What was the average number of absences during Week 1? Show your work.

   A. 23   C. 19.2
   B. 20.5   (D.) 17.6

2. What was the average number of absences on Fridays during this month? Show your work.

   (A.) 15.5   C. 27.1
   B. 14.8   D. 16

3. What was the range of absences for the month? Show your work.

   A. 10   (C.) 18
   B. 20   D. 23

4. Which day had the highest average number of absences? Show your work.

   (A.) Monday   C. Thursday
   B. Tuesday   D. Friday

© Carson-Dellosa CD-2212 | Total Problems: ____ Total Correct: ____ Score: ____ | **7**

Name _____

Study the example below. Write each number in standard numerical form on the line provided.

Example:

Two million, eight hundred sixty-thousand, one hundred twelve = **2,860,112**

1. Nine hundred fifty-seven _____

2. Eight thousand, five hundred forty-three _____

3. Forty-nine thousand, two hundred eleven _____

4. Three million, four hundred ninety-one thousand, eight _____

5. Seven million, fifty-one thousand, six hundred fourteen _____

6. One hundred thousand, three hundred twenty-six _____

7. Seven million, four hundred twenty-one thousand, fifteen _____

8. Eighty-nine thousand, six hundred ninety-five _____

9. Five billion, eight hundred forty million, three hundred thousand, one hundred fifty-five _____

10. Fifty million, two hundred sixty-two thousand, one hundred nine _____

11. Sixty thousand, four hundred three _____

12. Nine million, eight hundred forty-one thousand, seven hundred eighteen _____

13. Forty-six billion, eight thousand, fifty _____

14. Eleven thousand, four hundred twenty-six _____

15. Eight billion, five hundred sixteen million, three hundred five thousand, four hundred ninety-one _____

Total Problems:	Total Correct:	Score:

Name _____

Study the example below. Choose the number that is being expressed in expanded form. Circle the letter beside the correct answer.

Example:

$40,000 + 6,000 + 300 + 70 + 2 = \mathbf{46,372}$

1. $7,000 + 200 + 6 =$

   A. 7,206   B. 70,206   C. 726   D. 7,062

2. $9,000 + 400 + 30 + 5 =$

   A. 9,340   B. 945   C. 9,435   D. 90,435

3. $300,000 + 1,000 + 200 + 60 + 4 =$

   A. 300,164   B. 301,264   C. 310,264   D. 306,124

4. $900,000 + 70,000 + 600 + 30 + 8 =$

   A. 970,638   B. 97,638   C. 79,683   D. 9,007,638

5. $20,000,000 + 8,000,000 + 30,000 + 700 + 60 + 4 =$

   A. 20,830,764   B. 2,830,674   C. 20,837,064   D. 28,030,764

6. $1,000 + 80 + 3 =$

   A. 1,083   B. 10,803   C. 18,300   D. 1,038

7. $300,000 + 90,000 + 5,000 + 600 + 70 + 8 =$

   A. 309,568   B. 30,905,678   C. 395,678   D. 39,687

8. $10,000,000 + 8,000,000 + 70,000 + 3,000 + 400 + 40 + 4 =$

   A. 10,870,744   B. 1,873,444   C. 1,087,744   D. 18,073,444

10

Total Problems: _____   Total Correct: _____   Score: _____

Name _____

Circle the letter beside the correct answer.

1. Standard form for fifteen million, one hundred eight thousand, forty-one is:

   A. 15,841   C. 15,000,841

   B. 15,108,041   D. 1,510,841

2. Standard form for 60,000 + 3,000 + 500 + 40 + 6 is:

   A. 6,354   C. 63,546

   B. 603,546   D. 6,035,406

3. Find the number larger than 5,823.

   A. 5,863   C. 5,083

   B. 4,543   D. 5,423

4. Find the number 3,000 less than 978,653.

   A. 678,653   C. 975,653

   B. 948,653   D. 912,635

5. 4,768 in expanded form is:

   A. 400 + 700 + 60 + 8   C. 40,000 + 7,000 + 60 + 8

   B. 4,000 + 700 + 60 + 8   D. 4,000 + 7,000 + 60 + 8

6. 6,980,876 written in words is:

   A. six million, nine hundred eighty thousand, eight hundred sixty-seven

   B. six hundred eight thousand, eight hundred seventy-six

   C. six million, nine hundred eighty thousand, eight hundred seventy-six

   D. not given

7. What is ten thousand, four hundred twenty-seven in standard form?

   A. 10,427   C. 1,427

   B. 12,427   D. 10,027

Total Problems: **Total Correct:**   **Score:**

Study the example below. Look at the number given. Then, change the number according to the directions. Fill in the bubble to indicate whether the original number has been raised or lowered.

Example:

87,950:   Change the hundreds place value number to 7.

       Write the new number: **87,750**

       Was the number raised or lowered after the change?   Raised ◯   Lowered ●

---

1.   7,685:   Change the tens place value number to 4.

    Write the new number: _____   Raised ◯   Lowered ◯

2.   87,599:   Change the ten thousands place value number to 5.

    Write the new number: _____   Raised ◯   Lowered ◯

3.   734,238:   Change the hundreds place value number to 9.

    Write the new number: _____   Raised ◯   Lowered ◯

4.   569,042:   Change the ones place value number to 3.

    Write the new number: _____   Raised ◯   Lowered ◯

5.   674,313:   Change the hundreds place value number to 8.

    Write the new number: _____   Raised ◯   Lowered ◯

6.   70,435,675:   Change the millions place value number to 9.

    Write the new number: _____   Raised ◯   Lowered ◯

7.   554,876,908:   Change the thousands place value number to 4.

    Write the new number: _____   Raised ◯   Lowered ◯

8.   345,768:   Change the tens place value number to 7.

    Write the new number: _____   Raised ◯   Lowered ◯

Total Problems: _____   Total Correct: _____   Score: _____

Study the example below. Read each number. Then, using mental math, determine the new number with the information given. Write the answer on the line provided.

> **Example:**
>
> 45,289: Increase this number by 500.
>
> The new number is: **45,789**

1. 7,642: Decrease this number by 30. The new number is: _____

2. 65,908: Increase this number by 50. The new number is: _____

3. 5,879,903: Increase this number by 100,000. The new number is: _____

4. 34,588: Increase this number by 4,000. The new number is: _____

5. 40,786: Decrease this number by 30,000. The new number is:_____

6. 509,567: Increase this number by 20,000. The new number is: _____

7. 7,908,664: Decrease this number by 600,000. The new number is: _____

8. 5,897,442: Increase this number by 500. The new number is: _____

Total Problems:	Total Correct:	Score:

13

Add. Write the answer in the space provided.

1. 785
    + 17

2. 456
    + 123

3. 5,230
    + 503

4. 57,890
    + 23,678

5. 16,752
    + 3,584

6. 853,358
    + 571,453

7. 7,663
    + 9,023

8. 742,858
    + 531,693

Find the value of each missing number and write it in the box provided.

9. $15 + (5 + \boxed{}) = 9 + (8 + 8)$

10. $6 + (18 + 12) = \boxed{} + (17 + 9)$

11. $(8 + 2) + 15 = 7 + (13 + \boxed{})$

12. $(12 + 10) + 8 = (14 + 13) + \boxed{}$

13. $(11 + 7) + \boxed{} = (16 + 8) + 12$

14. $(20 + 3) + 18 = \boxed{} + (10 + 10)$

14

Total Problems:	Total Correct:	Score:

Name _____

Round each addend to the highest place value of the greater number. Add. Then, write the
answer in the space provided.

1.   43
    + 21

2.   64
    + 38

3.   99
    + 74

4.   231
    + 69

5.   382
    + 54

6.   787
    + 542

7.   2,609
    +   794

8.   3,588
    + 2,190

9.   34,871
    + 25,368

10.   45,043
    + 34,787

11.   236,708
    + 132,765

12.   567,908
    + 873,540

13.   897,654
    + 675,708

14.   1,765,342
    +   897,054

15.   3,008,765
    +   654,987

Total Problems: **Total Correct:**   **Score:**

Solve each word problem. Write the answer in the space provided.

1. Katie has 85 invitations to send for her party. She agreed to help a friend by writing 260 invitations to another party as well. How many invitations does Katie have to write in all?

5. Antoine and Dave are planning a trip. The first segment is 78 miles, the second is 123 miles, and the third is 147 miles. How many miles will they drive altogether?

2. Mark entered a bike-a-thon and rode 6 miles over the first two days, 9 miles the third day, and 7 miles the fourth day. How many miles did Mark ride in all for the bike-a-thon?

6. Maurice sold 54 bags of popcorn at the game on Saturday. He also sold 62 sodas. How many refreshment items did he sell in all?

3. Sonya swam 500 meters at practice on Monday and 700 meters on Tuesday. On Thursday she swam 350 meters. How many meters did she swim altogether?

7. Nell planted 16 bulbs, 15 marigolds, 18 begonias, and 4 geraniums. How many flowers did she plant in all?

4. Mrs. Warren sells newspaper subscriptions. Her goal each month is to sell 200 subscriptions. The first week she sold 87. Weeks two and three she sold 125 per week. Week four she sold 32. How many subscriptions did she sell altogether? Did she reach her goal?

8. Larry was in charge of seating one section of the auditorium. The first group he seated had 123 people in it. The second group had 87 people, and the third had 146 people. How many people did he seat in all?

16

Total Problems: _____   Total Correct: _____   Score: _____

Name _____

Subtract. Then, write the answer in the space provided.

1.
```
   76
 - 57
```

2.
```
   88
 - 36
```

3.
```
   525
 - 243
```

4.
```
   584
 - 129
```

5.
```
   725
 - 222
```

6.
```
   980
 - 764
```

7.
```
   1,858
 -   879
```

8.
```
   12,654
 -  3,569
```

9.
```
   287,327
 -  98,641
```

10.
```
   328,793
 -  54,317
```

11.
```
   897,562
 -  45,324
```

12.
```
   1,876,594
 -   733,982
```

13.
```
   4,956,233
 -   621,408
```

14.
```
   8,654,342
 -   458,336
```

15.
```
   8,721,607
 - 3,542,963
```

Total Problems:	Total Correct:	Score:

17

Round both numbers to the highest place value of the greater number. Subtract. Then, write the answer in the space provided.

1.   45
     − 19

2.   67
     − 39

3.   82
     − 67

4.   95
     − 58

5.   231
     − 74

6.   385
     − 97

7.   678
     − 239

8.   482
     − 166

9.   884
     − 159

10.   1,623
     − 1,407

11.   5,343
     − 2,567

12.   8,295
     − 4,597

13.   35,881
     − 22,567

14.   97,325
     − 72,654

15.   87,234
     − 58,585

16.   73,888
     − 29,742

17.   265,162
     − 139,790

18.   875,632
     − 338,517

19.   865,332
     − 728,661

20.   499,083
     − 225,668

18

| Total Problems: | Total Correct: | Score: |

Name _____

Solve each word problem. Write the answer in the space provided.

1. Marty had 156 new bicycle tires in his shop. He had 48 orders in one day for new tires. After filling the orders, how many tires did he have left?

2. Sheila started the day with 278 bottles of water at the refreshment tent. After the race, the runners had taken 246 bottles to drink. How many bottles of water did she have left?

3. Matt wrote a news article that had 987 words. His editor said he needed to shorten it to 684 words. How many words does he need to cut out of the news article?

4. Lakeisha bought 798 candy eggs for the egg hunt at the community park. After the egg hunt was over, only 743 eggs were found. How many eggs were not found?

5. Leandra and Bonnie made 467 picnic lunches for the campers. Two hundred thirty-four of them had ham sandwiches. The rest had turkey sandwiches. How many campers had turkey sandwiches?

6. Nicole had 79 minutes to have pictures developed before work. After 22 minutes, the photos were finished. How much time did she have left?

7. Mr. Freeman wanted 145 musicians in the school orchestra. He had 133 already signed up before the practices started. How many more musicians did he need for the performance?

8. Mary Beth baked 348 cookies for the school cafeteria. After all the lunches were served for the day, there were 78 cookies left over. How many cookies were served at lunch that day?

Total Problems: _____   Total Correct: _____   Score: _____

Multiply. Then, write the answer on the line provided.

1. $9 \times 6 =$ _____

2. $2 \times 3 =$ _____

3. $3 \times 5 =$ _____

4. $9 \times 2 =$ _____

5. $5 \times 5 =$ _____

6. $8 \times 5 =$ _____

7. $4 \times 8 =$ _____

8. $9 \times 5 =$ _____

9. $5 \times 2 =$ _____

10. $7 \times 8 =$ _____

11. $5 \times 12 =$ _____

12. $5 \times 4 =$ _____

13. $6 \times 7 =$ _____

14. $11 \times 7 =$ _____

15. $6 \times 4 =$ _____

16. $12 \times 6 =$ _____

17. $7 \times 9 =$ _____

18. $8 \times 8 =$ _____

19. $3 \times 4 =$ _____

20. $4 \times 7 =$ _____

21. $6 \times 3 =$ _____

22. $6 \times 5 =$ _____

23. $7 \times 7 =$ _____

24. $12 \times 3 =$ _____

25. $6 \times 6 =$ _____

26. $7 \times 5 =$ _____

27. $9 \times 4 =$ _____

28. $12 \times 12 =$ _____

29. $12 \times 9 =$ _____

30. $8 \times 2 =$ _____

31. $7 \times 10 =$ _____

32. $3 \times 8 =$ _____

33. $8 \times 10 =$ _____

34. $4 \times 4 =$ _____

35. $3 \times 7 =$ _____

36. $9 \times 9 =$ _____

Total Problems: **Total Correct:**   **Score:**

Name _____

Find the missing factor and write it on the line provided.

1. _____ x 4 = 32

5. _____ x 4 = 16

9. 7 x _____ = 28

2. 7 x _____ = 35

6. _____ x 6 = 24

10. _____ x 5 = 25

3. _____ x 9 = 36

7. _____ x 8 = 72

11. 8 x _____ = 56

4. _____ x 7 = 49

8. 9 x _____ = 54

12. 3 x _____ = 27

Solve to find the unknown amount. Work inside the parentheses first. Pay attention to the operation signs. Write the answer on the line provided.

13. (5 x 2) x 3 = _____

17. (3 x 3) + (8 x 2) = _____

14. (7 x 4) x _____ = 56

18. (3 x 4) + (7 x 7) = _____

15. (3 + 8) x 9 = _____

19. (2 x 7) – (3 x 1) = _____

16. (4 x 4) + (_____ x 2) = 26

20. (9 x 5) – 15 = _____

Total Problems:	Total Correct:	Score:

Multiply. Then, write the answer in the space provided.

1. 66
    x 10

2. 28
    x 12

3. 43
    x 16

4. 746
    x 85

5. 215
    x 28

6. 309
    x 19

7. 455
    x 76

8. 758
    x 93

9. 428
    x 27

10. 257
    x 66

11. 989
    x 49

12. 849
    x 79

13. 75
    x 19

14. 410
    x 67

15. 636
    x 73

16. 964
    x 83

Total Problems: _____ Total Correct: _____ Score: _____

Name _____

Multiply. Then, write the answer in the space provided.

1. 246 x 10	**5.** 752 x 60	**9.** 551 x 47	**13.** 221 x 24
2. 545 x 20	**6.** 958 x 64	**10.** 367 x 58	**14.** 119 x 68
3. 316 x 30	**7.** 862 x 37	**11.** 255 x 84	**15.** 401 x 97
4. 814 x 40	**8.** 377 x 42	**12.** 799 x 79	**16.** 655 x 18

Total Problems: **Total Correct:**   **Score:**

Name _____

Multiply. Then, write the answer in the space provided.

1. 44 x 2	**5.** 114 x 28	**9.** 306 x 247	**13.** 226 x 505
2. 75 x 18	**6.** 684 x 20	**10.** 528 x 458	**14.** 456 x 618
3. 86 x 37	**7.** 897 x 33	**11.** 654 x 856	**15.** 575 x 731
4. 94 x 36	**8.** 832 x 45	**12.** 740 x 160	**16.** 911 x 399

Total Problems: **Total Correct:** **Score:**

Name _____

Round each number to its highest place value. Multiply. Then, write the answer in the space provided.

1. 32
x 11

5. 233
x 49

9. 3,251
x 267

13. 8,759
x 202

2. 64
x 24

6. 546
x 40

10. 6,589
x 785

14. 11,528
x 243

3. 81
x 65

7. 859
x 67

11. 5,642
x 222

15. 9,095
x 186

4. 97
x 31

8. 747
x 36

12. 9,738
x 554

16. 26,305
x 1,172

Total Problems: ___ Total Correct: ___ Score: ___

Name _____

Solve. Write the answer on the line provided.

1. _____ x 7 = 28

2. 8 x 8 = _____

3. _____ x 4 = 16

4. _____ x 8 = 80

5. _____ x 4 = 16

6. 9 x 9 = _____

7. _____ x 5 = 30

8. 6 x 8 = _____

9. 3 x _____ = 36

10. _____ x 9 = 45

11. 5 x 5 = _____

12. 3 x _____ = 24

Solve by working inside the parentheses first. Write the answer on the line provided.

13. (9 + 7) x 10 = _____

14. (3 x 9) − 9 = _____

15. (8 x 2) x 1 = _____

16. (7 x 5) + (_____ x 2) = 43

Round each number to its highest place value. Multiply. Write the answer in the space provided.

17.
162
x 45
_____

18.
457
x 36
_____

19.
7,890
x 384
_____

Multiply. Write the answer in the space provided.

20.
456
x 31
_____

21.
784
x 62
_____

22.
957
x 50
_____

Total Problems: _____   Total Correct: _____   Score: _____

Solve each word problem. Write the answer in the space provided.

1. Wayne has played golf 3 hours a day for the past 23 days. How many hours has he played golf in all?

2. Veronica cuts 15 ladies' hair each day for 5 days. How many haircuts has she given after 5 days?

3. The Majestic Theater has 48 rows of seats. Each row has 25 seats. How many seats are there in all?

4. Rebecca glued 36 shamrocks on each section of the stage backdrop. There were 9 sections to the backdrop. How many shamrocks did she glue on the entire backdrop?

5. A bookstore received 18 boxes of a best-selling book. Each box holds 215 books. How many books did the bookstore receive?

6. Amy sold 15 necklaces each day for 12 days. How many necklaces did she sell in all?

7. Juan reads about 312 words per minute with excellent comprehension. If he reads for 30 minutes, how many words will he have read?

8. Monique's office has a coffee service. Each time the coffee is delivered, there is enough for 18 cups of coffee. If the service comes 20 times, and the office staff drinks all the available coffee each time, how many cups of coffee did the office staff drink during that period?

| Total Problems: | Total Correct: | Score: |

Name _____

Divide. Then, write the answer on the line provided.

1. $9 \div 3 =$ _____

2. $25 \div 5 =$ _____

3. $12 \div 4 =$ _____

4. $60 \div 5 =$ _____

5. $40 \div 8 =$ _____

6. $42 \div 6 =$ _____

7. $56 \div 8 =$ _____

8. $54 \div 6 =$ _____

9. $24 \div 4 =$ _____

10. $16 \div 8 =$ _____

11. $15 \div 3 =$ _____

12. $18 \div 6 =$ _____

13. $108 \div 9 =$ _____

14. $28 \div 7 =$ _____

15. $21 \div 7 =$ _____

16. $64 \div 8 =$ _____

17. $49 \div 7 =$ _____

18. $35 \div 7 =$ _____

19. $24 \div 3 =$ _____

20. $80 \div 8 =$ _____

Total Problems: _____   Total Correct: _____   Score: _____

Name _____

Solve the following number sentences. Always work inside the parentheses first. Then, write the answer on the line provided.

1. $(84 \div 7) + (9 \div 3) =$ _____

2. $(14 \div 2) - (15 \div 3) =$ _____

3. $(12 \div 4) \div 1 =$ _____

4. $(18 \div 2) + (16 \div 8) =$ _____

5. $(10 \div 5) +$ _____ $= 13$

6. $(20 \div 2) - (10 \div 5) =$ _____

7. $(50 \div 5) - (10 \div 2) =$ _____

8. $(36 \div 12) + (15 \div 3) =$ _____

9. $(25 \div 5) - (14 \div 7) =$ _____

10. $(108 \div 12) + (18 \div 2) =$ _____

Solve the following number sentences, where $\triangle = 5$. Write the answer on the line provided.

11. $(\triangle + 5) \div 10 =$ _____

12. $(15 \div \triangle) + (8 \div 2) =$ _____

13. $(24 \div 3) - \triangle =$ _____

14. $(90 \div \triangle) + (16 \div 8) =$ _____

15. $(85 \div 5) + \triangle =$ _____

16. $(100 \div 25) + \triangle + 7 =$ _____

17. $(60 \div \triangle) \div 6 =$ _____

18. $(30 \div \triangle) \div$ _____ $= 3$

19. $(70 \div \triangle) + (9 \div 3) =$ _____

20. $(26 - 13) - \triangle =$ _____

Total Problems: _____   Total Correct: _____   Score: _____

Name _____

Study the rule below. Divide. Then, write the answer in the space provided.

> **Rule:**
>
> Division is the opposite operation of multiplication.

1. $2\overline{)264}$

2. $8\overline{)648}$

3. $5\overline{)700}$

4. $6\overline{)240}$

5. $9\overline{)729}$

6. $3\overline{)126}$

7. $5\overline{)165}$

8. $7\overline{)847}$

9. $4\overline{)408}$

10. $6\overline{)426}$

11. $3\overline{)2,466}$

12. $8\overline{)3,288}$

13. $9\overline{)4,545}$

14. $7\overline{)4,914}$

15. $5\overline{)1,805}$

16. $6\overline{)3,612}$

17. $8\overline{)6,424}$

18. $9\overline{)8,199}$

19. $7\overline{)2,814}$

20. $4\overline{)2,600}$

30

Total Problems: **Total Correct:**   **Score:**

Name _____

Divide. Then, write the answer in the space provided.

1. $5\overline{)875}$

2. $3\overline{)7,982}$

3. $6\overline{)240}$

4. $7\overline{)5,014}$

5. $8\overline{)3,551}$

6. $4\overline{)7,668}$

7. $9\overline{)7,548}$

8. $5\overline{)1,025}$

9. $6\overline{)3,612}$

10. $12\overline{)426}$

11. $10\overline{)6,780}$

12. $8\overline{)19,577}$

13. $15\overline{)9,045}$

14. $8\overline{)32,865}$

15. $16\overline{)32,847}$

16. $5\overline{)75,020}$

Total Problems: **Total Correct:**   **Score:**

Name _____

Study the rule below. Round the dividend to its highest place value. Divide. Then, write the answer in the space provided.

Rule:

When estimating solutions to division problems, round the number in the dividend, then divide to get the estimated quotient.

1. $5\overline{)320}$

2. $3\overline{)882}$

3. $4\overline{)299}$

4. $6\overline{)5,559}$

5. $4\overline{)7,776}$

6. $9\overline{)8,562}$

7. $5\overline{)2,436}$

8. $2\overline{)4,224}$

9. $10\overline{)6,980}$

10. $10\overline{)1,160}$

11. $8\overline{)4,781}$

12. $4\overline{)7,890}$

Total Problems: _____ Total Correct: _____ Score: _____

Name _____

Solve each problem. Circle the letter beside the correct answer.

1. $8 \div 4 = \boxed{}$

   A. 3   C. 2

   B. 4   D. 6

2. $45 \div 9 = \boxed{}$

   A. 6   C. 7

   B. 5   D. 15

3. $70 \div 10 = \boxed{}$

   A. 7   C. 10

   B. 5   D. 4

4. $90 \div 5 = \boxed{}$

   A. 16   C. 18

   B. 15   D. 20

5. $7\overline{)497}$

   A. 70   C. 71

   B. 56   D. 64

6. $8\overline{)488}$

   A. 62   C. 60

   B. 61   D. 64

7. $9\overline{)4{,}237}$

   A. 477   C. 470 R7

   B. 527 R2   D. 479 R3

8. $45 \div 3 = \boxed{} + 7$

   A. 8   C. 13

   B. 15   D. 5

9. $(16 \div 4) + 6 = (20 \div \boxed{})$

   A. 3   C. 4

   B. 2   D. 5

10. $(25 \div 5) + \boxed{} = 15 + 15 + 5$

   A. 15   C. 35

   B. 30   D. 20

11. $(22 \div 11) + 8 = \boxed{} \div 2$

   A. 20   C. 60

   B. 200   D. 30

12. $(36 \div 3) + 8 = (200 \div \boxed{})$

   A. 2   C. 20

   B. 50   D. 10

Total Problems: **Total Correct:**   **Score:**

33

Solve each word problem. Write the answer in the space provided.

1. Miranda has 18 pieces of candy. She wants to give an equal number of pieces to her 6 friends. How many pieces of candy can each friend get?

2. Mr. Stanford wrote 64 pages of a travel brochure. He wants to divide it into 8 equal sections. How many pages will be in each section?

3. Melanie's trip was 498 miles long. She drove the same number of miles each day for 3 days. How many miles did she drive each day?

4. Latoya bought a new rack for her CD collection. She has 976 CDs. Each row of the rack holds 12 CDs. How many rows can she fill? Will there be any partially filled rows?

5. Yolanda opened 280 cans of tomato sauce for a restaurant. For one pan of lasagna, 4 cans of sauce are needed. How many pans of lasagna could she make if Yolanda uses all of the cans?

6. Mr. Thompson cut the grass on the golf course in 1,680 minutes. How many hours did it take to mow the grass?

7. Mark ran 873 miles his first year in the track club. If Mark ran 9 miles each time, how many times did he run during the year?

8. Kevin and his father have collected 1,456 different coins over the years. They have a coin album that holds 30 coins on a page. If they put the coins in the album, how many pages will they use? Will there be any pages partially filled?

34

| Total Problems: | Total Correct: | Score: |

Name _____

Study the rules below. Complete each problem.

Rules:	Examples: $\frac{2}{3}$ is in simplest form.
A fraction is in simplest form if the denominator and the numerator have no common factors greater than 1.	$\frac{5}{10} = \frac{5 \div 5}{10 \div 5} = \frac{1}{2}$
Find equivalent fractions by dividing the denominator and numerator by a **common** factor.	The simplest form of $\frac{5}{10}$ is $\frac{1}{2}$.

1. $\frac{4}{8} = \frac{}{2}$

2. $\frac{13}{52} = \frac{}{4}$

3. $\frac{6}{16} = \frac{}{8}$

4. $\frac{15}{35} = \frac{3}{}$

5. $\frac{8}{10} = \frac{4}{}$

6. $\frac{9}{54} = \frac{1}{}$

7. $\frac{8}{64} = \frac{}{8}$

8. $\frac{7}{56} = \frac{}{8}$

Write each fraction in its simplest form in the space provided.

9. $\frac{12}{15} =$

10. $\frac{6}{8} =$

11. $\frac{25}{100} =$

12. $\frac{5}{40} =$

13. $\frac{7}{77} =$

14. $\frac{4}{36} =$

15. $\frac{18}{20} =$

16. $\frac{100}{1,000} =$

Total Problems:	Total Correct:	Score:

35

Name _____

Study the examples below.

Examples:

How to make an improper fraction: $6\frac{2}{3}$

1. Multiply the denominator and the whole number.   ➤ $3 \times 6 = 18$

2. Add the product to the numerator.   ➤ $18 + 2 = 20$

3. Place the answer over the denominator.   ➤ $\frac{20}{3}$

How to make a mixed number: $\frac{20}{3}$

1. Divide the numerator by the denominator.

$$3\overline{)20}$$
$$-\ 18$$
$$\overline{2}$$

2. Write the quotient as the whole number.

3. The remainder is written as the numerator over the denominator (divisor).

$6\frac{2}{3}$

Write the mixed number as an improper fraction in the space provided.

1. $12\frac{1}{5} =$

2. $5\frac{5}{8} =$

3. $9\frac{7}{9} =$

4. $8\frac{2}{4} =$

5. $9\frac{5}{9} =$

6. $10\frac{6}{8} =$

Write the improper fraction as a mixed number in the space provided.

7. $\frac{27}{4} =$

8. $\frac{19}{6} =$

9. $\frac{23}{6} =$

10. $\frac{126}{25} =$

11. $\frac{50}{7} =$

12. $\frac{64}{9} =$

36

Total Problems:	Total Correct:	Score:

Name _____

Study the box below. Add or subtract. Write the sum or difference in simplest form in the space provided.

Rule:	**Example:** $\dfrac{1}{2} + \dfrac{1}{10} =$
1. Find a common denominator when adding or subtracting fractions with unlike denominators.	$\dfrac{1\ (\times 5)}{2\ (\times 5)} = \dfrac{5}{10}$
2. For each fraction, multiply the numerator by the same factor as the denominator.	$+\ \dfrac{1\ (\times 1)}{10\ (\times 1)} = \dfrac{1}{10}$
3. Use the renamed fractions to solve the problem. Reduce if necessary.	$\dfrac{6}{10} = \dfrac{3}{5}$

1. $\dfrac{4}{9} + \dfrac{1}{3} =$

2. $\dfrac{5}{10} + \dfrac{2}{5} =$

3. $\dfrac{5}{6} - \dfrac{3}{18} =$

4. $\dfrac{8}{9} - \dfrac{2}{3} =$

5. $\dfrac{3}{5} - \dfrac{3}{7} =$

6. $\dfrac{8}{9} - \dfrac{1}{6} =$

7. $\dfrac{1}{2} + \dfrac{2}{3} =$

8. $\dfrac{1}{5} + \dfrac{4}{15} =$

9. $\dfrac{7}{8} - \dfrac{3}{4} =$

10. $\dfrac{4}{11} + \dfrac{2}{3} =$

Total Problems: _____   Total Correct: _____   Score: _____

37

Study the examples below. Find the sum or difference. Remember to find a common denominator before adding or subtracting. Simplify your answer in the space provided.

Examples:

$$\frac{3}{8} + \frac{4}{8} = \frac{7}{8} \longleftarrow \quad (3 + 4 = 7)$$

$$\frac{7}{12} - \frac{4}{8} = \quad \begin{array}{c} \dfrac{7\ (\times\ 2)}{12\ (\times\ 2)} = \dfrac{14}{24} \\[8pt] -\ \dfrac{4\ (\times\ 3)}{8\ (\times\ 3)} = \dfrac{12}{24} \\ \hline \dfrac{2}{24} = \dfrac{1}{12} \end{array}$$

1. $\dfrac{2}{3} - \dfrac{1}{3} =$

2. $\dfrac{5}{6} - \dfrac{1}{3} =$

3. $\dfrac{4}{9} + \dfrac{1}{3} =$

4. $\dfrac{5}{10} + \dfrac{2}{5} =$

5. $\dfrac{3}{5} + \dfrac{9}{10} =$

6. $\dfrac{3}{5} + \dfrac{4}{9} =$

7. $\dfrac{5}{9} - \dfrac{2}{9} =$

8. $\dfrac{5}{6} - \dfrac{3}{18} =$

9. $\dfrac{3}{7} + \dfrac{2}{3} =$

10. $\dfrac{5}{6} - \dfrac{3}{6} =$

11. $\dfrac{4}{11} + \dfrac{2}{3} =$

12. $\dfrac{9}{14} - \dfrac{3}{7} =$

13. $\dfrac{2}{7} + \dfrac{5}{14} =$

14. $\dfrac{2}{3} - \dfrac{1}{6} =$

15. $\dfrac{13}{16} - \dfrac{5}{16} =$

16. $\dfrac{10}{15} - \dfrac{2}{10} =$

17. $\dfrac{3}{4} + \dfrac{1}{2} =$

18. $\dfrac{2}{3} + \dfrac{5}{7} =$

19. $\dfrac{2}{3} + \dfrac{1}{6} =$

20. $\dfrac{3}{4} - \dfrac{1}{12} =$

Total Problems: _____   Total Correct: _____   Score: _____

Name _____

Complete each problem. Then, write the answer in the space provided.

1. $6\frac{1}{2} - 1\frac{3}{4} =$

2. $15\frac{1}{6} - 11\frac{7}{10} =$

3. $9\frac{2}{5} - 8\frac{1}{2} =$

4. $10\frac{1}{3} - 1\frac{2}{3} =$

5. $8\frac{3}{10} - 2\frac{7}{10} =$

6. $15\frac{2}{3} - 3\frac{3}{4} =$

7. $17\frac{3}{6} - 13\frac{5}{6} =$

8. $19\frac{1}{2} - 8\frac{2}{3} =$

9. $17\frac{2}{3} - 8\frac{1}{9} =$

10. $15\frac{1}{2} - 14 =$

11. $13\frac{7}{8} - 1\frac{3}{4} =$

12. $10\frac{7}{9} - 9\frac{1}{3} =$

13. $18\frac{7}{8} - 1\frac{3}{4} =$

14. $9 - 8\frac{1}{2} =$

15. $16\frac{3}{10} - 13\frac{5}{6} =$

16. $2\frac{1}{10} - 1\frac{1}{6} =$

17. $14\frac{5}{6} - 12\frac{1}{2} =$

18. $14\frac{1}{2} - 7 =$

19. $16\frac{2}{3} - 3 =$

20. $13\frac{1}{3} - 6\frac{1}{2} =$

21. $3\frac{2}{5} - 1\frac{1}{5} =$

| Total Problems: | Total Correct: | Score: |

Study the box below. Multiply. Write the answer in simplest form in the space provided.

Rule:	Example:
1. Multiply the numerators.	
2. Multiply the denominators.	$\dfrac{1}{3} \times \dfrac{3}{10} = \dfrac{3}{30} = \dfrac{1}{10}$
3. Write the product in simplest form.	

1. $\dfrac{2}{3} \times \dfrac{5}{7} =$

2. $\dfrac{4}{7} \times \dfrac{2}{9} =$

3. $\dfrac{3}{8} \times \dfrac{3}{4} =$

4. $\dfrac{5}{6} \times \dfrac{2}{5} =$

5. $\dfrac{2}{4} \times \dfrac{1}{2} =$

6. $\dfrac{5}{9} \times \dfrac{1}{5} =$

7. $\dfrac{1}{2} \times \dfrac{4}{9} =$

8. $\dfrac{2}{3} \times \dfrac{3}{10} =$

9. $\dfrac{1}{3} \times \dfrac{5}{6} =$

10. $\dfrac{1}{8} \times \dfrac{1}{10} =$

11. $\dfrac{2}{7} \times \dfrac{1}{3} =$

12. $\dfrac{4}{5} \times \dfrac{7}{8} =$

13. $\dfrac{2}{7} \times \dfrac{5}{9} =$

14. $\dfrac{2}{3} \times \dfrac{3}{5} =$

15. $\dfrac{7}{9} \times \dfrac{1}{2} =$

40

Total Problems: _____   Total Correct: _____   Score: _____

Name _____

Study the example below. Multiply. Write each product in simplest form in the space provided.

Rule:	Example: $5\frac{1}{4} \times \frac{2}{3} =$
To multiply mixed numbers: 1. Make the mixed number an improper fraction. Multiply the two fractions. 2. Simplify the answer.	$\frac{21}{4} \times \frac{2}{3} = \frac{42}{12}$ $\frac{42}{12} = 3\frac{6}{12} = 3\frac{1}{2}$

1. $1\frac{1}{3} \times \frac{2}{3} =$

2. $8\frac{2}{5} \times 3\frac{1}{8} =$

3. $4\frac{1}{2} \times \frac{2}{3} =$

4. $\frac{2}{5} \times 5\frac{1}{2} =$

5. $\frac{1}{2} \times 6\frac{2}{3} =$

6. $2\frac{1}{2} \times 2\frac{1}{3} =$

7. $6 \times 3\frac{3}{4} =$

8. $8\frac{2}{5} \times \frac{1}{2} =$

9. $1\frac{1}{6} \times 4\frac{3}{4} =$

10. $2\frac{1}{4} \times 3\frac{2}{3} =$

11. $\frac{3}{8} \times 4\frac{2}{3} =$

12. $12\frac{1}{5} \times 4\frac{2}{15} =$

Total Problems: ___   Total Correct: ___   Score: ___   41

Solve each word problem. Write the answers in the space provided.

1. Warren harvested $\frac{3}{5}$ of the corn crop in the morning. After lunch, Warren harvested the other $\frac{2}{5}$ of the crop. How much more was harvested in the morning?

4. Jimmy, John, and Abbey went to buy fruit. Jimmy bought $\frac{1}{2}$ pound of grapes. John bought $\frac{3}{4}$ of a pound of bananas. Abbey bought $4\frac{1}{4}$ pounds of oranges. How much was the total weight of their bags of fruit?

2. Jerry and Thomas own a cleaning business. Thomas cleans a house in $2\frac{1}{2}$ hours. Jerry cleans a house in $3\frac{1}{4}$ hours. How much longer does it take Jerry to clean a house than Thomas?

5. Roger collected 5 dozen eggs to sell at the market. If Roger sold $\frac{2}{3}$ of the eggs, how many did he sell?

3. Kelly makes fruit juice each morning. She uses $2\frac{1}{3}$ pints of strawberries and $1\frac{2}{5}$ pints of grapes in her juice. If she doubles her recipe, how many more pints of strawberries than pints of grapes will she use?

6. Corey wants to buy grass seed for his yard, which measures 252 square feet. Each bag of grass seed covers 12 square feet. What fraction of his yard will one bag of seed cover?

Total Problems: _____   **Total Correct:** _____   **Score:** _____

Name _____

Study the rule below. Write each number as a decimal in the space provided.

Rule:

tens	ones		tenths	hundredths	thousandths
8	7	.	5	4	9

The decimal point separates the whole number from the parts of the whole.
Read this number as: **eighty-seven and five hundred forty-nine-thousandths**
Write this number as a decimal: **87.549**

1. six and twenty-three-thousandths

2. four and seventy-six-hundredths

3. four hundred thirty-thousandths

4. fifty-three-thousandths

5. fifty-three-hundredths

6. twenty-nine and five-thousandths

Write the words for each decimal in the space provided.

7. 6.789

8. 0.293

9. 2,929.874

10. 9.768

11. 0.600

12. 0.003

13. 4.510

14. 2,000.02

Write the value of the underlined digit on the line provided.

15. 0.00<u>7</u> _____

16. 2.0<u>8</u>7 _____

17. 75.<u>8</u>54 _____

18. 12<u>7</u>.90 _____

19. 3,897.00<u>3</u> _____

20. 12.7<u>3</u>8 _____

21. 437.0<u>4</u> _____

22. <u>3</u>,543.21 _____

Total Problems:	Total Correct:	Score:

43

Study the examples below. Add or subtract. Line up the decimal points when you rewrite the problem vertically. Write the answer in the space provided.

Examples:	53.89 + 50.37 =	43.89 − 22.78 =
	Rewrite the addition problem vertically.	Rewrite the subtraction problem vertically.

$$\begin{array}{r} \overset{1\ \ 1}{53.89} \\ +\ \ 50.37 \\ \hline 104.26 \end{array}$$
Line up the decimal points. Add each place value and carry as needed.

$$\begin{array}{r} 43.89 \\ -\ 22.78 \\ \hline 21.11 \end{array}$$
Line up the decimal points. Subtract each place value and borrow as needed.

1. $10.10 + 3.56 =$

2. $7.79 − 5.34 =$

3. $567.009 − 65.87 =$

4. $654.90 + 87.09 =$

5. $48.23 + 93.9 =$

6. $87.09 − 9.02 =$

7. $60.87 − 23.1 =$

8. $12.322 + 1.003 =$

9. $19.3 − 8 =$

10. $942.35 + 1.233 =$

11. $400 − .98 =$

12. $34.1 + .413 =$

13. $67.9 − 7.9 =$

14. $14.87 + .09 =$

15. $9.76 + 7.99 =$

16. $56.9 + 8.9 + 6.3 =$

17. $876.09 − 45.8 =$

18. $5.8 + 9.7 + 5.1 =$

19. $700 − .08 =$

20. $2.349 + 482.2 =$

21. $0.87 − 0.54 =$

Total Problems: _____ Total Correct: _____ Score: _____

Name _____

Study the example below. Multiply. Write the answer in the space provided.

Example:

	Multiply as you would with whole numbers.		Count the number of digits to the right of the decimal point.		Keep the same number of digits to the right of the decimal point in the product.
$\begin{array}{r} ^{4\,7} \\ 14.8 \\ \times\ \ 9 \\ \hline 1332 \end{array}$		$\begin{array}{r} ^{4\,7} \\ 14.\mathbf{8} \\ \times\ \ 9 \\ \hline 1332 \end{array}$		$\begin{array}{r} ^{4\,7} \\ 14.8 \\ \times\ \ 9 \\ \hline 133.\mathbf{2} \end{array}$	

1. $\begin{array}{r} 78 \\ \times\ 7.9 \\ \hline \end{array}$

5. $87 \times 5.867 =$

9. $35 \times 6.9 =$

13. $\begin{array}{r} 6.29 \\ \times\ 0.5 \\ \hline \end{array}$

2. $\begin{array}{r} 11.735 \\ \times\ \ \ \ 78 \\ \hline \end{array}$

6. $0.9 \times 476.7 =$

10. $124 \times 9.5 =$

14. $0.54 \times 6.13 =$

3. $\begin{array}{r} 49 \\ \times\ 0.8 \\ \hline \end{array}$

7. $\begin{array}{r} 8.756 \\ \times\ \ \ 6.8 \\ \hline \end{array}$

11. $576 \times 9.64 =$

15. $0.5 \times 57.54 =$

4. $49 \times 8.097 =$

8. $\begin{array}{r} 69 \\ \times\ 5.9 \\ \hline \end{array}$

12. $\begin{array}{r} 59.4 \\ \times\ .08 \\ \hline \end{array}$

16. $8.47 \times 0.33 =$

Total Problems: _____ Total Correct: _____ Score: _____

45

Study the example below. Divide. Then, write the answer in the space provided.

Example:

$$3\overline{)49.2}$$

$$\begin{array}{r} 16. \\ 3\overline{)49.2} \\ -3 \\ \hline 19 \\ -18 \\ \hline 1 \end{array}$$

Divide the whole number.

Place the decimal point in the quotient.

$$\begin{array}{r} 16.4 \\ 3\overline{)49.2} \\ -3 \\ \hline 19 \\ -18 \\ \hline 12 \\ -12 \\ \hline 0 \end{array}$$

Divide the tenths.

$49.2 \div 3 = \textbf{16.4}$

1. $39.33 \div 9 =$

4. $91.117 \div 43 =$

7. $7.260 \div 20 =$

2. $21.265 \div 5 =$

5. $1.644 \div 3 =$

8. $6.850 \div 50 =$

3. $27.768 \div 78 =$

6. $51.36 \div 12 =$

9. $87.966 \div 27 =$

| Total Problems: | Total Correct: | Score: |

Name _____

Study the example below. Write the decimal on the line provided.

Example:

(4 parts out of 10 are shaded.)

Decimal   Fraction

four-tenths = **0.4**   four-tenths = $\dfrac{4}{10}$

---

1. two-fifths = _____

2. two-fourths = _____

3. three-tenths = _____

4. nine-tenths = _____

5. $\dfrac{3}{4}$ = _____

6. $\dfrac{6}{12}$ = _____

7. $\dfrac{12}{100}$ = _____

8. $\dfrac{36}{100}$ = _____

Write the fraction on the line provided.

9. one-fourth = _____

10. three-fifths = _____

11. twenty-one-hundredths = _____

12. fourteen-hundredths = _____

13. .25 = _____

14. .04 = _____

15. .9 = _____

16. .30 = _____

Total Problems:	Total Correct:	Score:

47

Solve each word problem. Write the answer in the space provided.

1. Gail's anemometer measures the wind speed at 44.14 kilometers per hour, 4 times faster than the wind speed 5 hours ago. What was the wind speed 5 hours ago?

2. One of the heaviest rainfalls ever recorded in a 24-hour period was 178.80 centimeters. If the rainfall was constant, how much rain fell during each hour?

3. In a 50-meter swimming race, four swimmers had these times: 35.2 seconds, 31.2 seconds, 33.4 seconds, 29.8 seconds. Was their combined time faster or slower than 2 minutes 30 seconds?

4. Gas costs $1.24 per gallon. Ruth's car holds 10 gallons. She fills her tank 3 times. How much does Ruth spend for gas?

5. Carol uses an average of 291.4 kilowatt-hours of electricity each month. Carol pays $0.18 per kilowatt hour. What is Carol's average monthly bill?

6. Kenny bought a shirt for $58.98. The sales tax was $3.54. Kenny gave the clerk a $100.00 bill. How much change did the clerk give Kenny?

Total Problems: _____ Total Correct: _____ Score: _____

Name _____

Study the box below. Write each ratio three different ways in the space provided.

Rule:	Example:
A **ratio** compares two quantities.	7 bananas to 9 monkeys $\frac{7}{9}$ 7:9 7 to 9 This ratio can be written three ways.

1. 4 balls to 12 bats

2. 14 boys to 24 girls

3. 16 classrooms to 56 schools

4. 2 polar bears to 4 giraffes

5. 7 socks to 10 shoes

6. 9 tigers to 12 lions

7. 7 apples to 19 pears

8. 5 comedies to 10 dramas

Study the box below. Determine whether each pair of ratios is equal. Write "yes" or "no" in the space provided.

Rule:	Example:
To determine if ratios are **equal,** cross multiply. If the products are equal, the ratios are equal.	$(1 \times 3 = 3)$ $\frac{1}{2}$ ⤬ $\frac{2}{3}$ $(2 \times 2 = 4)$ $3 \neq 4$ **Not an equal ratio.**

9. $\frac{5}{6}, \frac{10}{11}$

10. $\frac{3}{8}, \frac{6}{16}$

11. $\frac{6}{5}, \frac{7}{6}$

12. $\frac{8}{20}, \frac{1}{5}$

13. $\frac{3}{4}, \frac{5}{15}$

14. $\frac{4}{5}, \frac{8}{10}$

15. $\frac{24}{30}, \frac{15}{30}$

16. $\frac{2}{3}, \frac{8}{12}$

17. $\frac{3}{4}, \frac{2}{3}$

Total Problems:	Total Correct:	Score:

49

Study the box below. Write each percent as a fraction. Simplify each fraction. Then, write the answer in the space provided.

Rule:	Example:
A percent is a ratio that compares a quantity to 100.	85 correct questions to 100 total questions
	$85\% = \dfrac{85}{100} = \dfrac{17}{20}$

1.	86%	**6.**	60%	**11.**	81%	**16.**	99%
2.	95%	**7.**	20%	**12.**	8%	**17.**	48%
3.	75%	**8.**	25%	**13.**	5%	**18.**	24%
4.	68%	**9.**	30%	**14.**	35%	**19.**	29%
5.	10%	**10.**	73%	**15.**	42%	**20.**	45%

Total Problems: **Total Correct:**   **Score:**

Name _____

Study the examples below. Find the percent for each number using one of the two methods. Then, write the answer in the space provided.

Examples:	Method One: using fractions	Method Two: using decimals
$75\% = \dfrac{75}{100} = \dfrac{3}{4}$	75% of 60 $\dfrac{3}{4}$ x 60 equals **45**	75% of 60 .75 x 60 equals **45**

1. 25% of 4

2. 50% of 44

3. 70% of 450

4. 90% of 660

5. 75% of 20

6. 10% of 100

7. 8% of 720

8. 55% of 480

9. 25% of 100

10. 90% of 30

11. 76% of 100

12. 4% of 200

13. 33% of 200

14. 40% of 100

15. 50% of 30

16. 5% of 65

17. 10% of 520

18. 35% of 70

Total Problems: _____ **Total Correct:** _____ **Score:** _____

Solve each problem. Circle the letter beside the correct answer.

1. What is 25% of 450?

   A. 112.50

   B. 112

   C. 125

   D. not given

3. A 100-seat studio has 32 empty seats. What percent of the studio's seats are full?

   A. 50%

   B. 65%

   C. 68%

   D. not given

2. What is another way of representing the following ratio?

   $$19 : 15$$

   A. $\dfrac{15}{19}$ C. $\dfrac{5}{9}$

   B. $1\dfrac{4}{15}$ D. not given

4. Find the missing number:

   $$\frac{6}{9} = \frac{48}{n}$$

   A. $n = 6$

   B. $n = 54$

   C. $n = 72$

   D. not given

Total Problems: _____   Total Correct: _____   Score: _____

Name _____

Solve each word problem. Write the answer in the space provided.

1. Pia's class planned a hiking trip during spring break. Only 30% of Pia's class went on the trip. If there were 60 people in her class, how many people went hiking?

3. A total of 541 passengers bought tickets from Fly-Away Airways in four days. If 143 flew on the first and third days and 255 flew on the fourth day, how many flew on the second day?

2. Fred has $250.00 to spend for his summer vacation. He budgeted 20% of his money for souvenirs. How much money did he budget for souvenirs?

4. Travis is driving from Kansas City to Dallas on business. He drives at a rate of 95 miles every 2 hours. How far would he drive in 3 hours?

Name _____

Find each time. All times for problems 1 through 6 are P.M. Write the answer on the line provided.

1. 35 minutes after

_____

3. 45 minutes after

_____

5. 5 minutes before

_____

2. 15 minutes before

_____

4. 20 minutes after

_____

6. 35 minutes before

_____

---

7. What time is 15 minutes after 7:25 P.M.?

_____

9. What time will it be 4 hours and 5 minutes after 8:35 P.M.?

_____

11. Add 15 minutes to 4:18 P.M. to get a new time.

_____

8. What time is 3 hours and 25 minutes before 1:45 A.M.?

_____

10. How much time has elapsed between 9:36 P.M. and 2:45 A.M.?

_____

12. What is 1 hour and 25 minutes before 3:05 P.M.?

_____

Total Problems:	Total Correct:	Score:

Use the schedule to answer the questions. Then, write your answer on the line provided.

Train 101 New Haven, CT to New York, NY		**Train 202** Atlanta, GA to Charlotte, NC		**Train 300** Dallas, TX to Santa Fe, NM	
Departs	Arrives	Departs	Arrives	Departs	Arrives
6:00 A.M.	7:30 A.M.	5:00 P.M.	8:45 P.M.	11:00 A.M.	1:00 P.M.

1. How long is the trip from Atlanta to Charlotte? _____

2. What time does Train 300 leave Dallas? _____

3. To what city does Train 101 travel? _____

4. When does Train 101 arrive in New York? _____

5. Which train goes to Charlotte? _____

6. Which train leaves the earliest? _____

7. Which train has the longest trip? _____

8. Which train(s) depart in the morning? _____

9. How many hours does the trip to Santa Fe take? _____

10. Which train departs at 5:00 P.M.? _____

Total Problems:	Total Correct:	Score:

Use the calendars to answer the questions. Then, write the answer on the line provided.

March

Sun.	Mon.	Tues.	Wed.	Thurs.	Fri.	Sat.
1	2	3	4	5	6	7
8	9	10	11	12	13	14
15	16	17	18	19	20	21
22	23	24	25	26	27	28
29	30	31				

April

Sun.	Mon.	Tues.	Wed.	Thurs.	Fri.	Sat.
			1	2	3	4
5	6	7	8	9	10	11
12	13	14	15	16	17	18
19	20	21	22	23	24	25
26	27	20	29	30		

1. What is the date of the second Tuesday in March? _____

2. On what day of the week does April begin? _____

3. On what day does March 17 fall? _____

4. What date is the fourth Friday in March? _____

5. What day of the week is the seventh day of April? _____

6. How many days is it from March 26 to April 3? _____

7. How many Tuesdays are between March 18 and April 17? _____

8. How many Sundays are in April? _____

56

Total Problems: _____   Total Correct: _____   Score: _____

Name _____

Solve each word problem. Write the answer in the space provided.

1. Marcus wants to go to work 1 hour and 40 minutes early on Monday. He usually goes to work at 7:30 A.M. What time will he go to work on Monday?

2. Nathan went to the ball game at 5:45 P.M. He returned to his house 3 hours and 50 minutes after he left. What time did he return?

3. Melissa wanted to attend her sister's soccer game at 3:30 and see a movie that starts at 4:15. If the game lasts 50 minutes, will she be on time for the movie?

4. Jarron and Kyle rode their bikes for 2 hours and 24 minutes. They left Kyle's house at 4:00 P.M. What time did they return?

5. Selina went to baby-sit at 5:00 P.M. Saturday night. The parents returned at 9:30 P.M. How long did Selina baby-sit that evening?

6. Mr. Miller left his office at 7:15 P.M. He went to the gym for 1 hour and 20 minutes and to the store for another 32 minutes. Then, he went home. What time did Mr. Miller arrive home?

7. Amy left for her friend's birthday party at 1:20 P.M. It took her mother 24 minutes to drive to the girl's house. What time did Amy arrive at the party?

8. The Coastal Drink Factory opens for employees at 6:00 A.M. and closes at 11:30 P.M. How many hours is the business open each day?

Total Problems: _____   Total Correct: _____   Score: _____

Study the examples below. Estimate. Then, find the actual sums and differences, compare to each estimate, and write the answer in the space provided.

Examples:

Round to the nearest $0.**10**.	Round to the nearest $**1**.00.	Round to the nearest $**10**.00.
$0.85 $\longrightarrow$ .90 +0.29 $\longrightarrow$ .30 **$1.20**	$8.39 $\longrightarrow$ 8.00 + 2.75 $\longrightarrow$ 3.00 **$11.00**	$34.60 + $47.30 = $30.00 + $50.00 = **$80.00**

1. $302.76 + $98.57 =

5. $1.34 + $4.56 =

9.
$49.64
26.05
9.98
+ 73.02

2.
$63.89
− 24.23

6. $77.29 − $9.58 =

10.
$7.74
− 5.46

3.
$32.51
17.25
+ 9.62

7.
$18.25
14.45
+ 6.56

11.
$6.59
8.25
+ 1.45

4.
$1,501.69
− 928.72

8. $45.78 − $26.09 =

12.
$38.74
29.07
+ 56.86

Total Problems: Total Correct: Score:

Name _____

Study the box below. Complete each problem in the space provided. Be sure to place the numbers in the correct place value and watch the placement of the decimal point.

Rule:		Example: $3.76	
$165.28 + 163.20 $328.48	If there are 2 numbers to the right of the decimal, there should be 2 numbers to the right of the decimal point in the product.	$$4\overline{)15.04}$$ $$\begin{array}{r} -12 \\ \hline 30 \\ -28 \\ \hline 24 \\ -24 \\ \hline 0 \end{array}$$	Place the decimal point in the quotient. It goes in the same place as in the dividend.

1. $264.98 x 9 =

2. $18.79 x 8 =

3. $113.96 ÷ 4 =

4. $42.36 x 12 =

5. $149.94 ÷ 6 =

6. $92.82 x 21 =

7. $124.02 ÷ 9 =

8. $171.24 ÷ 12 =

Total Problems: _____ Total Correct: _____ Score: _____

59

Solve each word problem. Then, write the answer in the space provided. Where appropriate, write the dollar sign and the decimal (cent) point in the answer.

1. Jake has $15.00 to spend for a Mother's Day gift. He wants to buy roses. They cost $2.50 each. How many roses can Jake purchase?

4. Sean went to a hockey game. He spent $6.79 on food, $15.27 on a souvenir puck, and $27.68 on the ticket. How much money did he spend all together?

2. Sharon went shopping for a surprise birthday party. She spent $14.23 on balloons, $29.61 on a gift, and $28.32 for food. How much did she spend in all?

5. Kyle earns $42.78 each week for delivering newspapers. He delivered newspapers for 8 weeks. How much money did Kyle earn in 8 weeks?

3. Last year, Carla earned $1,023.59 by cutting grass and doing odd jobs for neighbors. This year, she earned $1,562.22. How much more did Carla earn this year?

6. Kristi wants to buy 3 shirts for $18.99 each. If she has $75.00, how much money will she have left after buying the shirts?

Total Problems: _____   Total Correct: _____   Score: _____

Name _____

Study the rules below. Write inches, feet, yards, or miles as appropriate on the line provided.

Rules:	Customary Units	
	12 inches (in) = 1 foot (ft)	1,760 yd = 1 mile (mi)
	3 ft = 1 yard (yd)	5,280 ft = 1 mi

1. The width of a doorway may be 49 _____ .

2. My father's height is about 6 _____ tall.

3. I jumped 46 _____ in the standing long jump.

4. Each morning, I run about 5 _____ for exercise.

5. I threw the softball 20 _____ to reach home plate.

6. A desk might be 46 _____ wide.

7. The distance from Atlanta, GA, to Harrisburg, PA, is about 845 _____ .

8. The height of my stuffed animal is $7\frac{1}{2}$ _____ .

9. The width of my television is 36 _____ .

Choose the appropriate unit of measurement. Write inches (in), feet (ft), yards (yd), or miles (mi) on the line provided.

10. length of a football field: _____

11. distance to Mars: _____

12. distance you throw a ball: _____

13. thickness of a textbook: _____

Complete. Write the answer on the line provided.

14. 18 ft = _____ in

15. 5 ft 3 in = _____ in

16. 440 yd = _____ mi

17. 10,560 ft = _____ mi

18. 36 in = _____ ft

19. 120 in = _____ ft

Total Problems:	Total Correct:	Score:

Name _____

Study the rules below. Write ounces, pounds, or tons as appropriate on the line provided.

> **Rules:**　　　Customary Units
>
> 16 ounces (oz)　=　1 pound (lb)
> 2,000 pounds (lb)　=　1 ton (t)

1. An elephant may weigh 2 _____ .

2. A glass of juice may weigh 6 _____ .

3. A car weighs about 1 _____ .

4. A cat weighs about 9 _____ .

Choose the appropriate unit of measurement. Write ounces (oz), pounds (lb), or tons (t) on the line provided.

5. the weight of a potato chip: _____

6. the weight of a truck: _____

7. the weight of a pair of shoes: _____

8. the weight of a key: _____

Complete. Write the answer on the line provided.

9. 224 oz = _____ lb

10. 80 oz = _____ lb

11. 4 lb = _____ oz

12. 2 t = _____ lb

13. 16,000 lb = _____ t

14. 5 t = _____ oz

15. 8 lb = _____ oz

16. 500 lb = _____ t

17. 1.5 lb = _____ oz

Total Problems: _____　　Total Correct: _____　　Score: _____

Name _____

Study the rules below. Write cups, pints, quarts, or gallons as appropriate on the line provided.

Rules:	Customary Units	
	2 cups (c) = 1 pint (pt)	4 qt = 1 gallon (gal)
	2 pt = 1 quart (qt)	16 c = 1 gal

Choose the appropriate unit of measurement. Write cups (c), pints (pt), quarts (qt), or gallons (gal) on the line provided.

1. measuring milk for a brownie mix: _____

4. measuring a barrel's capacity: _____

2. gasoline needed for a car: _____

5. a bowl of soup: _____

3. water for a swimming pool: _____

6. a milk jug: _____

Complete. Write the answer on the line provided.

7. 2 gal = _____ qt

11. 3 gal = _____ qt

15. 2 pt = _____ c

8. 4 pt = _____ qt

12. 3 gal + 2 qt = _____ c

16. 5 qt = _____ pt

9. 6 c = _____ pt

13. _____ pt = 2 qt

17. _____ gal = 16 pt

10. 8 qt = _____ gal

14. 3 c = _____ pt

18. 5 gal = _____ qt

Name _____

Study the rules below. Choose the appropriate metric unit of measurement. Write millimeters (mm), centimeters (cm), meters (m), or kilometers (km) on the line provided.

> **Rules:**   Metric Units
>
> 10 millimeters (mm) = 1 centimeter (cm)
>
> 100 cm = 1 meter (m)
>
> 1,000 m = 1 kilometer (km)

1. A car travels at 55 _____ per hour.

2. A thumbtack is 4 _____ long.

3. A man is about 2 _____ tall.

4. A pen is 15 _____ long.

Choose the appropriate unit of measurement. Write millimeters (mm), centimeters (cm), meters (m), or kilometers (km) on the line provided.

5. the length of a soccer field: _____

6. the distance to the sun: _____

7. a day's ride in the car: _____

8. the length of a straw: _____

9. the width of a pencil eraser: _____

10. the length of a classroom: _____

11. the width of a foot: _____

12. the distance to run a marathon: _____

Complete. Write the answer on the line provided.

13. 48 km = _____ m

14. 835.7 cm = _____ mm

15. 0.01 m = _____ cm

16. 3 km = _____ m

17. 93 cm = _____ m

18. 756 mm = _____ m

19. 7,007 mm = _____ cm

20. 54 km = _____ cm

Total Problems:	Total Correct:	Score:

Name _____

Study the rules below. Choose the appropriate unit of measurement. Write grams (g), milligrams (mg), or kilograms (kg) on the line provided.

Rules: Metric Units
1,000 milligrams (mg) = 1 gram (g)
1,000 g = 1 kilogram (kg)

1. A gold bracelet might weigh 11

   _____ .

2. A quarter might weigh 3 _____ .

3. A vitamin tablet might weigh 100

   _____ .

4. An adult might weigh 90 _____ .

Choose the appropriate unit of measurement. Write grams (g), milligrams (mg), or kilograms (kg) on the line provided.

5. a nickel: _____

6. a bicycle: _____

7. a new pencil: _____

8. a gold necklace: _____

9. an orange: _____

10. a sewing needle: _____

11. a kitchen table: _____

12. a paper clip: _____

Complete. Write the answer on the line provided.

13. 3,200 g = _____ kg

14. _____ g = 8 kg

15. 3,000 mg = _____ g

16. 6,000 mg = _____ kg

17. 7 kg = _____ mg

18. 7 kg = _____ g

19. 14 kg = _____ g

20. 64 g = _____ mg

Total Problems: _____   Total Correct: _____   Score: _____

65

Study the rule below. Then, use the chart to complete the questions. Circle the letter beside the correct answer.

Rule:

To convert Celsius (C°) to Fahrenheit (F°), multiply the Celsius temperature by 1.8 and add 32.

To convert Fahrenheit (F°) to Celsius (C°), subtract 32 from the Fahrenheit temperature, multiply the difference by 5, then divide the product by 9.

Fahrenheit Thermometer

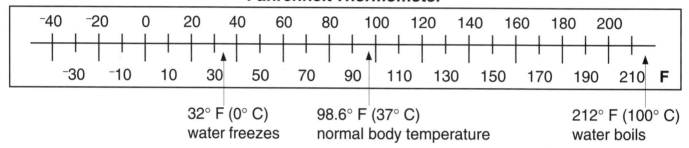

32° F (0° C)
water freezes

98.6° F (37° C)
normal body temperature

212° F (100° C)
water boils

1. The temperature on a snowy day might be _____.

   A. 23° F   C. 80° F
   B. 50° F   D. 70° F

2. The temperature of a cold drink might be _____.

   A. 12° C   C. 40° C
   B. ⁻10° C   D. 0° C

3. The temperature on a hot August day might be _____.

   A. 93° F   C. 55° F
   B. 34° F   D. 50° F

4. A cup of hot chocolate might be _____.

   A. ⁻5° C   C. 80° C
   B. 8° C   D. 110° C

5. The temperature of swimming pool water during the summer might be _____.

   A. 39° C   C. 78° C
   B. ⁻35° C   D. 140° C

6. A home located near the equator might have an average temperature of _____.

   A. 30° C   C. 0° C
   B. 95° C   D. 10° C

7. The temperature of a warm slice of pizza might be _____.

   A. 80° F   C. 213° F
   B. 35° F   D. 15° F

8. The temperature of a child with a fever might be _____.

   A. 38° C   C. 20° C
   B. 0° C   D. 110° C

Total Problems: _____   Total Correct: _____   Score: _____

Solve each word problem. Write the answer in the space provided.

1. Gary bakes 10 loaves of bread for the party. He needs 4 cups of milk for each loaf. How many quarts of milk does he need to bake all of the loaves?

2. Elizabeth needs $1\frac{1}{2}$ gallons of water to water her plants. Her watering can holds 1 quart. How many times will Elizabeth fill her watering can to water her plants?

3. Matthew delivered 7 containers of orange juice to the Apple Tree Restaurant. Each container had 8 quarts of orange juice. How many gallons of orange juice did Matthew deliver?

4. Demarcus buys 9 gallons of ice cream for his birthday party. He has 34 guests coming. If each guest eats $2\frac{1}{2}$ cups of ice cream, how many pints of ice cream will be left over?

5. Evelyn's swimming pool requires 3 quarts of a bacteria-cleaning agent 5 times a month. How many gallons of this agent will Evelyn use during June, July, and August?

6. Neal changed the oil in his vehicle. The car required 6 quarts of oil. If Neal wants to change his oil every month for a year, how many quarts of oil will Neal need?

Study the rules below. Name the polygons. Then, write the answer on the line provided.

Rules:	**Vocabulary:**	prefix	# of sides
A four-sided figure is called a **quadrilateral.**	A **polygon** is a closed figure that has three or more straight line segments.	penta	5
		hexa	6
	A **closed figure** is a figure that has no open line segments. You can trace a line around the perimeter of a closed figure without ever coming to an end.	hepta	7
		octa	8
		nona	9
		deca	10

1.
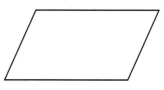
_____

5.

_____

2.
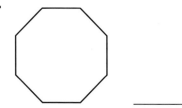
_____

6.

_____

3.
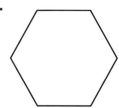
_____

7.
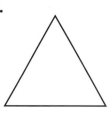
_____

4.
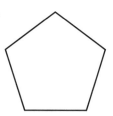
_____

8.

_____

Total Problems: _____   Total Correct: _____   Score: _____

Name _____

Study the rules below. Identify angles as right, acute, obtuse, or straight. Then, write the
answer on the line provided.

Rules:

Right Angle	**Acute Angle**	**Obtuse Angle**	**Straight Angle**
A right angle measures exactly 90 degrees.	An acute angle measures less than 90 degrees.	An obtuse angle measures more than 90 degrees but less than 180 degrees.	A straight angle measures exactly 180 degrees.
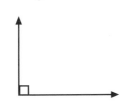			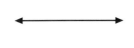

1.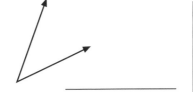
_____

2.
_____

3.
_____

4.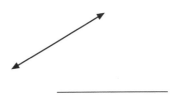
_____

5.
_____

6.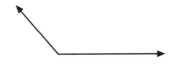
_____

7.
_____

8.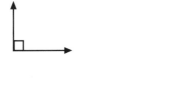
_____

9.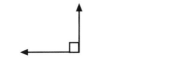
_____

10.
_____

11.
_____

12.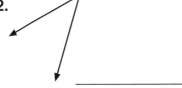
_____

Total Problems:	Total Correct:	Score:

Study the rules below. Write the type of triangle shown on each line provided.

Rules:

Equilateral Triangle An equilateral triangle has all three sides of equal length. 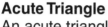	**Isoceles Triangle** At least two sides of an isoceles triangle are of equal length.	**Scalene Triangle** Each side of a scalene triangle is a different length. 
Right Triangle A right triangle has one right angle.	**Acute Triangle** An acute triangle has three acute angles.	**Obtuse Triangle** An obtuse triangle has one obtuse angle.

1.  _____

2. _____

3.  _____

4. 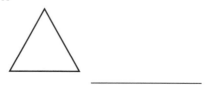 _____

5. _____

6. _____

7.  _____

8.  _____

9. 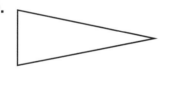 _____

10.  _____

11. _____

12.  _____

Total Problems:	Total Correct:	Score:

Name _____

Study the rules below. Write chord, diameter, or radius for the given segment on the line provided.

Rules:

A **chord** is a line segment that has its endpoints on the circle.

A **diameter** is a chord that passes through the center of a circle.

A **radius** is a line segment that has one endpoint on the circle and one endpoint on the center of the circle.

1. 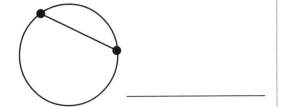 _____

4. 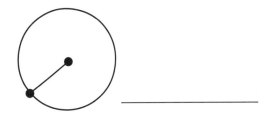 _____

2.  _____

5. 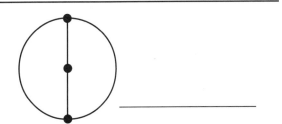 _____

3. 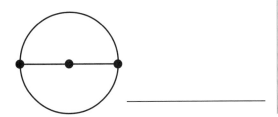 _____

6. 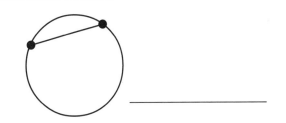 _____

Fill in the table. Remember that the radius is half the diameter.

	7.	8.	9.	10.	11.	12.
Diameter	10 cm	_____	25 mm	_____	44 m	_____
Radius	_____	9 in	_____	14 mm	_____	7.5 yd

Total Problems: _____ Total Correct: _____ Score: _____

Name _____

Study the box below. Find the perimeter of each figure and write it on the line provided.

Rule:	Example: 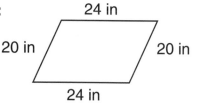
The **perimeter** of a figure is the distance around it. This can be found by adding the measurements of all sides together.	24 + 20 + 24 + 20 = **88** **perimeter = 88 inches**

1.

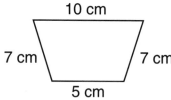

_____

2.

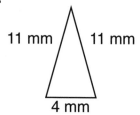

_____

3.

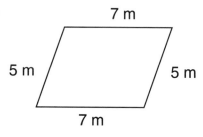

_____

4.

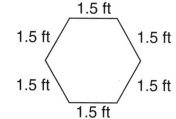

_____

5.

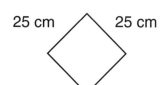

_____

6.

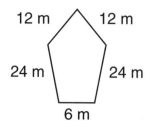

_____

Total Problems:	Total Correct:	Score:

Name _____

Study the box below. Multiply to find the area of the rectangle or square. Write the answer in the space provided.

Rule:	Example:
The **area** of a figure is the number of square units it contains. To find the area, count square units or multiply the length times the width.	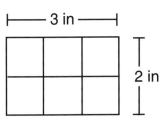

Rule:

The **area** of a figure is the number of square units it contains. To find the area, count square units or multiply the length times the width.

Area of a square or rectangle = length x width

A = l x w

Example:

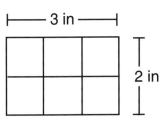

A = 3 in x 2 in

A = 6 square inches or 6 in²

1. l = 7 mm, w = 4 mm

2. l = 16 ft, w = 12 ft

3. l = 21 cm, w = 15 cm

4. l = 13 mi, w = 8 mi

5. l = 50 ft, w = 15 ft

6. l = 34 m, w = 33 m

7. l = 15 in, w = 98 in

8. l = 67 mi, w = 12 mi

9. l = 53 km, w = 12 km

10. l = 9 m, w = 23 m

11. l = 19 in, w = 29 in

12. l = 89 cm, w = 57 cm

Total Problems: Total Correct: Score:

Solve each word problem. Write the answer in the space provided.

1. This figure shows the amount of space needed to build a new playground. If the perimeter is 65 feet, what is the missing measurement?

15 ft

30 ft

4. Delaney's swimming pool is the shape of a rectangle. The length equals 18 yards and the width equals 10 yards. What size pool cover will Delaney need to buy to cover the pool?

2. Circle A has a diameter of 75 meters and circle B has a radius of 45 meters. Which circle is wider?

5. Charles wants to buy 425 sq. miles of land. If each sq. mile costs $1,200.00, how much money does Charles need to buy the land?

3. A new softball field is being built. The seats will go around three-fourths of the field. If the total perimeter is 2,400 yards, what is the total amount of space needed for the seats?

6. Is this figure a polygon?

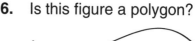
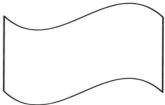

Total Problems: _____   Total Correct: _____   Score: _____

Name _____

Use the information in the table to answer the questions. Write the answers on the lines provided.

Fly-Away Airlines Destination Cities

April	May	June	July	August
Chicago, IL	Birmingham, AL	Miami, FL	Dallas, TX	Reno, NV
New York, NY	Dallas, TX	New York, NY	Chicago, IL	New York, NY
Miami, FL	Reno, NV	Washington, DC	Cleveland, OH	Salt Lake City, UT
Atlanta, GA	Boise, ID	Baltimore, MD	Las Vegas, NV	Dallas
Baltimore, MD	Newark, NJ	Atlanta, GA	Toronto, ON	Newark

1. When does the airline go to Reno? _____

2. How many times during the five-month period will there be flights to Dallas? _____

3. What month(s) offer flights to Toronto? _____

4. Other than April, when is there a flight to Chicago? _____

5. Which months do not have a flight to Dallas scheduled? _____

6. During the five months, how many flights are there to Birmingham? _____

7. Other than Cleveland and Las Vegas, what other cities are available to fly into in July?

   _____

8. Which months offer Newark as a destination? _____

9. Flights to Atlanta are offered in which month(s)? _____

10. How many different cities will the airline fly to in the five months? _____

Total Problems:	Total Correct:	Score:

Use the line graph to answer the questions. Write the answer in the space provided.

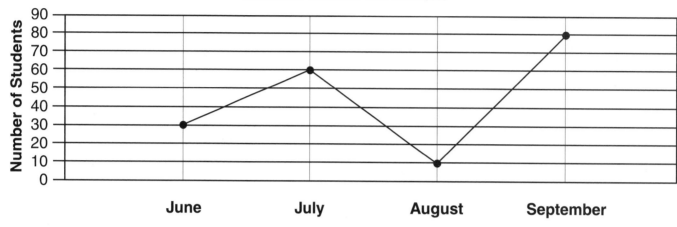

1. According to the line graph, did enrollment in summer school increase or decrease from June to August?

2. What was the difference in enrollment from the beginning to the end of the summer?

3. How many students were enrolled during June, July, and August?

4. If it cost $45.90 for each student for school supplies, how much money was needed during September?

5. Each student had to bring $20.00 for art supplies. How much money did the school collect for art supplies over the entire summer?

6. For every 10 students, there must be a teacher. How many teachers were needed in July?

Total Problems: _____ Total Correct: _____ Score: _____

Name _____

Study the box below. Fill in the chart with the mean, median, mode, and range for the following groups of numbers.

Rules:	Examples:
The **mean** (average) is found by adding the numbers and dividing by the number of addends.	$26 + 26 + 54 + 57 + 60 = 223$ $223 \div 5 = 44.6$ **mean = 44.6**
The **median** is the number in the middle of a sequential list of numbers. If there is no middle number, the median is the average of the two middle numbers in the list.	26, 26, 54, 57, 60 **median = 54**
The **mode** is the number that appears most often.	26, 26, 54, 57, 60 **mode = 26**
The **range** is the difference between the greatest number and the least number.	26, 26, 54, 57, 60 $60 - 26 = 34$ **range = 34**

NUMBERS	MEAN	MEDIAN	MODE	RANGE
1. 2, 4, 9, 10, 23, 23, 43				
2. 15, 15, 17, 18, 19, 23, 31				
3. 19, 19, 34, 34, 34, 67, 85				
4. 84, 84, 89, 91, 94				
5. 39, 71, 73, 74, 74, 83, 84				

Total Problems: **Total Correct:** **Score:**

Name _____

Probability

Study the examples below. Using the given information, answer the questions in the space provided.

Examples:

Stopping on black
Favorable outcomes: 1
Possible outcomes: 4

Probability: $\frac{1}{4}$

Stopping on white
Favorable outcomes: 3
Possible outcomes: 4

Probability: $\frac{3}{4}$

The image on the right is a spinner. The spinner has been spun and lands on white. The probability of stopping on white is: $\frac{3}{4}$

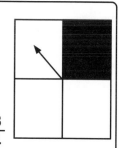

A S S E S S M E N T

Use these letter cards to answer the problems below.

1. Write the ratio for the probability of picking the letter **S.**

4. Write the ratio for the probability of picking a consonant.

2. Write the ratio for the probability of picking the letter **E.**

5. Write the ratio for the probability of picking the letter **N.**

3. Write the ratio for the probability of picking a vowel.

6. Write the ratio for the probability of picking the letter **M.**

78

Total Problems: _____ Total Correct: _____ Score: _____

© Carson-Dellosa CD-2212

Reading and Writing Numbers

Name _____

Study the example below. Write each number in standard numerical form on the line provided.

> **Example:**
> Two million, eight hundred sixty-thousand, one hundred twelve = **2,860,112**

1. Nine hundred fifty-seven — 957
2. Eight thousand, five hundred forty-three — 8,543
3. Forty-nine thousand, two hundred eleven — 49,211
4. Three million, four hundred ninety-one thousand, eight — 3,491,008
5. Seven million, fifty-one thousand, six hundred fourteen — 7,051,614
6. One hundred thousand, three hundred twenty-six — 100,326
7. Seven million, four hundred twenty-one thousand, fifteen — 7,421,015
8. Eighty-nine thousand, six hundred ninety-five — 89,695
9. Five billion, eight hundred forty million, three hundred thousand, one hundred fifty-five — 5,840,300,155
10. Fifty million, two hundred sixty-two thousand, one hundred nine — 50,262,109
11. Sixty thousand, four hundred three — 60,403
12. Nine million, eight hundred forty-one thousand, seven hundred eighteen — 9,841,718
13. Forty-six billion, eight thousand, fifty — 46,000,008,050
14. Eleven thousand, four hundred twenty-six — 11,426
15. Eight billion, five hundred sixteen million, three hundred five thousand, four hundred ninety-one — 8,516,305,491

Total Problems:	Total Correct:	Score:	**9**

© Carson-Dellosa CD-2212

Expanded Form

Name _____

Study the example below. Choose the number that is being expressed in expanded form. Circle the letter beside the correct answer.

> **Example:**
> 40,000 + 6,000 + 300 + 70 + 2 = **46,372**

1. 7,000 + 200 + 6 =
   (A) 7,206   B. 70,206   C. 726   D. 7,062

2. 9,000 + 400 + 30 + 5 =
   A. 9,340   B. 945   (C) 9,435   D. 90,435

3. 300,000 + 1,000 + 200 + 60 + 4 =
   A. 300,164   (B) 301,264   C. 310,264   D. 306,124

4. 900,000 + 70,000 + 600 + 30 + 8 =
   (A) 970,638   B. 97,638   C. 79,683   D. 9,007,638

5. 20,000,000 + 8,000,000 + 30,000 + 700 + 60 + 4 =
   A. 20,830,764   B. 2,830,674   C. 20,837,064   (D) 28,030,764

6. 1,000 + 80 + 3 =
   (A) 1,083   B. 10,803   C. 18,300   D. 1,038

7. 300,000 + 90,000 + 5,000 + 600 + 70 + 8 =
   A. 309,568   B. 30,905,678   (C) 395,678   D. 39,687

8. 10,000,000 + 8,000,000 + 70,000 + 3,000 + 400 + 40 + 4 =
   A. 10,870,744   B. 1,873,444   C. 1,087,744   (D) 18,073,444

10	Total Problems:	Total Correct:	Score:

© Carson-Dellosa CD-2212

Mixed Practice

Name _____

Circle the letter beside the correct answer.

1. Standard form for fifteen million, one hundred eight thousand, forty-one is:
   A. 15,841   C. 15,000,841
   (B) 15,108,041   D. 1,510,841

2. Standard form for 60,000 + 3,000 + 500 + 40 + 6 is:
   A. 6,354   (C) 63,546
   B. 603,546   D. 6,035,406

3. Find the number larger than 5,823.
   (A) 5,863   C. 5,083
   B. 4,543   D. 5,423

4. Find the number 3,000 less than 978,653.
   A. 678,653   (C) 975,653
   B. 948,653   D. 912,635

5. 4,768 in expanded form is:
   A. 400 + 700 + 60 + 8   C. 40,000 + 7,000 + 60 + 8
   (B) 4,000 + 700 + 60 + 8   D. 4,000 + 7,000 + 60 + 8

6. 6,980,876 written in words is:
   A. six million, nine hundred eighty thousand, eight hundred sixty-seven
   B. six hundred eight thousand, eight hundred seventy-six
   (C) six million, nine hundred eighty thousand, eight hundred seventy-six
   D. not given

7. What is ten thousand, four hundred twenty-seven in standard form?
   (A) 10,427   C. 1,427
   B. 12,427   D. 10,027

Total Problems:	Total Correct:	Score:	**11**

© Carson-Dellosa CD-2212

Place Value

Name _____

Study the example below. Look at the number given. Then, change the number according to the directions. Fill in the bubble to indicate whether the original number has been raised or lowered.

> **Example:**
> 87,950: Change the hundreds place value number to 7.
> Write the new number: **87,750**
> Was the number raised or lowered after the change?   Raised ○   Lowered ●

1. 7,685: Change the tens place value number to 4.
   Write the new number: 7,645   Raised ○   Lowered ●

2. 87,599: Change the ten thousands place value number to 5.
   Write the new number: 57,599   Raised ○   Lowered ●

3. 734,238: Change the hundreds place value number to 9.
   Write the new number: 734,938   Raised ●   Lowered ○

4. 569,042: Change the ones place value number to 3.
   Write the new number: 569,043   Raised ●   Lowered ○

5. 674,313: Change the hundreds place value number to 8.
   Write the new number: 674,813   Raised ●   Lowered ○

6. 70,435,675: Change the millions place value number to 9.
   Write the new number: 79,435,675   Raised ●   Lowered ○

7. 554,876,908: Change the thousands place value number to 4.
   Write the new number: 554,874,908   Raised ○   Lowered ●

8. 345,768: Change the tens place value number to 7.
   Write the new number: 345,778   Raised ●   Lowered ○

12	Total Problems:	Total Correct:	Score:

© Carson-Dellosa CD-2212

Worksheet 13 — Mental Math

Name _____ Mental Math

Study the example below. Read each number. Then, using mental math, determine the new number with the information given. Write the answer on the line provided.

Example:
45,289: Increase this number by 500.
The new number is: **45,789**

1. 7,642: Decrease this number by 30. The new number is: **7,612**
2. 65,908: Increase this number by 50. The new number is: **65,958**
3. 5,879,903: Increase this number by 100,000. The new number is: **5,979,903**
4. 34,588: Increase this number by 4,000. The new number is: **38,588**
5. 40,786: Decrease this number by 30,000. The new number is: **10,786**
6. 509,567: Increase this number by 20,000. The new number is: **529,567**
7. 7,908,664: Decrease this number by 600,000. The new number is: **7,308,664**
8. 5,897,442: Increase this number by 500. The new number is: **5,897,942**

© Carson-Dellosa CD-2212 · Total Problems: · Total Correct: · Score: · **13**

Worksheet 14 — Addition Review

Name _____ Addition Review

Add. Write the answer in the space provided.

1. 785 + 17 = **802**
3. 5,230 + 503 = **5,733**
5. 16,752 + 3,584 = **20,336**
7. 7,663 + 9,023 = **16,686**
2. 456 + 123 = **579**
4. 57,890 + 23,678 = **81,568**
6. 853,358 + 571,453 = **1,424,811**
8. 742,858 + 531,693 = **1,274,551**

Find the value of each missing number and write it in the box provided.

9. 15 + (5 + [**5**]) = 9 + (8 + 8)
12. (12 + 10) + 8 = (14 + 13) + [**3**]
10. 6 + (18 + 12) = [**10**] + (17 + 9)
13. (11 + 7) + [**18**] = (16 + 8) + 12
11. (8 + 2) + 15 = 7 + (13 + [**5**])
14. (20 + 3) + 18 = [**21**] + (10 + 10)

14 · Total Problems: · Total Correct: · Score: · © Carson-Dellosa CD-2212

Worksheet 15 — Addition Estimation

Name _____ Addition Estimation

Round both addends to the highest place value of the greater number. Add. Then, write the answer in the space provided.

1. 43 + 21 → 40 + 20 = 60
2. 64 + 38 → 60 + 40 = 100
3. 99 + 74 → 100 + 100 = 200
4. 231 + 69 → 200 + 100 = 300
5. 382 + 54 → 400 + 100 = 500
6. 787 + 542 → 800 + 500 = 1,300
7. 2,609 + 794 → 3,000 + 1,000 = 4,000
8. 3,588 + 2,190 → 4,000 + 2,000 = 6,000
9. 34,871 + 25,368 → 30,000 + 30,000 = 60,000
10. 45,043 + 34,787 → 50,000 + 30,000 = 80,000
11. 236,708 + 132,765 → 200,000 + 100,000 = 300,000
12. 567,908 + 873,540 → 600,000 + 900,000 = 1,500,000
13. 897,654 + 675,708 → 900,000 + 700,000 = 1,600,000
14. 1,765,342 + 897,054 → 2,000,000 + 1,000,000 = 3,000,000
15. 3,008,765 + 654,987 → 3,000,000 + 1,000,000 = 4,000,000

© Carson-Dellosa CD-2212 · Total Problems: · Total Correct: · Score: · **15**

Worksheet 16 — Problem Solving with Addition

Name _____ Problem Solving with Addition

Solve each word problem. Write the answer in the space provided.

1. Katie has 85 invitations to send for her party. She agreed to help a friend by writing 260 invitations to another party as well. How many invitations does Katie have to write in all?
85 + 260 = 345 invitations

2. Mark entered a bike-a-thon and rode 6 miles over the first two days, 9 miles the third day, and 7 miles the fourth day. How many miles did Mark ride in all for the bike-a-thon?
6 + 9 + 7 = 22 miles

3. Sonya swam 500 meters at practice on Monday and 700 meters on Tuesday. On Thursday she swam 350 meters. How many meters did she swim altogether?
500 + 700 + 350 = 1,550 meters

4. Mrs. Warren sells newspaper subscriptions. Her goal each month is to sell 200 subscriptions. The first week she sold 87. Weeks two and three she sold 125 per week. Week four she sold 32. How many subscriptions did she sell altogether? Did she reach her goal?
87 + 125 + 125 + 32 = 369 subscriptions; Yes

5. Antoine and Dave are planning a trip. The first segment is 78 miles, the second is 123 miles, and the third is 147 miles. How many miles will they drive altogether?
78 + 123 + 147 = 348 miles

6. Maurice sold 54 bags of popcorn at the game on Saturday. He also sold 62 sodas. How many refreshment items did he sell in all?
54 + 62 = 116 refreshment items

7. Nell planted 16 bulbs, 15 marigolds, 18 begonias, and 4 geraniums. How many flowers did she plant in all?
16 + 15 + 18 + 4 = 53 flowers

8. Larry was in charge of seating one section of the auditorium. The first group he seated had 123 people in it. The second group had 87 people, and the third had 146 people. How many people did he seat in all?
123 + 87 + 146 = 356 people

16 · Total Problems: · Total Correct: · Score: · © Carson-Dellosa CD-2212

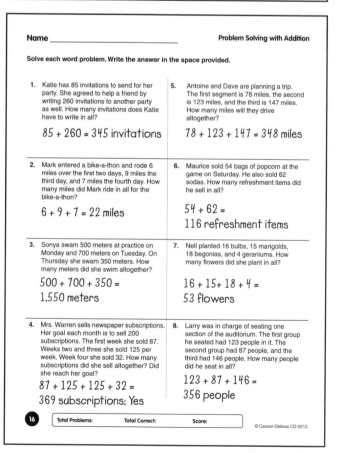

Worksheet 1 (top left)

Name _____   Subtraction Review

Subtract. Then, write the answer in the space provided.

1.	76 − 57 = 19	6.	980 − 764 = 216	11.	897,562 − 45,324 = 852,238
2.	88 − 36 = 52	7.	1,858 − 879 = 979	12.	1,876,594 − 733,982 = 1,142,612
3.	525 − 243 = 282	8.	12,654 − 3,569 = 9,085	13.	4,956,233 − 621,408 = 4,334,825
4.	584 − 129 = 455	9.	287,327 − 98,641 = 188,686	14.	8,654,342 − 458,336 = 8,196,006
5.	725 − 222 = 503	10.	328,793 − 54,317 = 274,476	15.	8,721,607 − 3,542,963 = 5,178,644

Total Problems: ___ Total Correct: ___ Score: ___   **17**

© Carson-Dellosa CD-2212

Worksheet 2 (top right)

Name _____   Subtraction Estimation

Round both numbers to the highest place value of the greater number. Subtract. Then, write the answer in the space provided.

1.	45 − 19 → 50 − 20 = 30	6.	385 − 97 → 400 − 100 = 300	11.	5,343 − 2,567 → 5,000 − 3,000 = 2,000	16.	73,888 − 29,742 → 70,000 − 30,000 = 40,000
2.	67 − 39 → 70 − 40 = 30	7.	678 − 239 → 700 − 200 = 500	12.	8,295 − 4,597 → 8,000 − 5,000 = 3,000	17.	265,162 − 139,790 → 300,000 − 100,000 = 200,000
3.	82 − 67 → 80 − 70 = 10	8.	482 − 166 → 500 − 200 = 300	13.	35,881 − 22,567 → 40,000 − 20,000 = 20,000	18.	875,632 − 338,517 → 900,000 − 300,000 = 600,000
4.	95 − 58 → 100 − 60 = 40	9.	884 − 159 → 900 − 200 = 700	14.	97,325 − 72,654 → 100,000 − 70,000 = 30,000	19.	865,332 − 728,661 → 900,000 − 700,000 = 200,000
5.	231 − 74 → 200 − 100 = 100	10.	1,623 − 1,407 → 2,000 − 1,000 = 1,000	15.	87,234 − 58,585 → 90,000 − 60,000 = 30,000	20.	499,083 − 225,668 → 500,000 − 200,000 = 300,000

18   Total Problems: ___ Total Correct: ___ Score: ___

© Carson-Dellosa CD-2212

Worksheet 3 (bottom left)

Name _____   Problem Solving with Subtraction

Solve each word problem. Write the answer in the space provided.

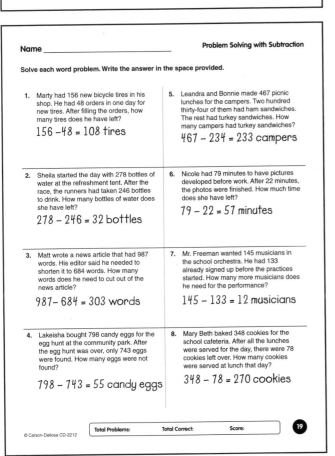

1. Marty had 156 new bicycle tires in his shop. He had 48 orders in one day for new tires. After filling the orders, how many tires does he have left?

   156 − 48 = 108 tires

2. Sheila started the day with 278 bottles of water at the refreshment tent. After the race, the runners had taken 246 bottles to drink. How many bottles of water does she have left?

   278 − 246 = 32 bottles

3. Matt wrote a news article that had 987 words. His editor said he needed to shorten it to 684 words. How many words does he need to cut out of the news article?

   987 − 684 = 303 words

4. Lakeisha bought 798 candy eggs for the egg hunt at the community park. After the egg hunt was over, only 743 eggs were found. How many eggs were not found?

   798 − 743 = 55 candy eggs

5. Leandra and Bonnie made 467 picnic lunches for the campers. Two hundred thirty-four of them had ham sandwiches. The rest had turkey sandwiches. How many campers had turkey sandwiches?

   467 − 234 = 233 campers

6. Nicole had 79 minutes to have pictures developed before work. After 22 minutes, the photos were finished. How much time does she have left?

   79 − 22 = 57 minutes

7. Mr. Freeman wanted 145 musicians in the school orchestra. He had 133 already signed up before the practices started. How many more musicians does he need for the performance?

   145 − 133 = 12 musicians

8. Mary Beth baked 348 cookies for the school cafeteria. After all the lunches were served for the day, there were 78 cookies left over. How many cookies were served at lunch that day?

   348 − 78 = 270 cookies

Total Problems: ___ Total Correct: ___ Score: ___   **19**

© Carson-Dellosa CD-2212

Worksheet 4 (bottom right)

Name _____   Basic Multiplication Facts

Multiply. Then, write the answer on the line provided.

1.	9 x 6 = 54	19.	3 x 4 = 12
2.	2 x 3 = 6	20.	4 x 7 = 28
3.	3 x 5 = 15	21.	6 x 3 = 18
4.	9 x 2 = 18	22.	6 x 5 = 30
5.	5 x 5 = 25	23.	7 x 7 = 49
6.	8 x 5 = 40	24.	12 x 3 = 36
7.	4 x 8 = 32	25.	6 x 6 = 36
8.	9 x 5 = 45	26.	7 x 5 = 35
9.	5 x 2 = 10	27.	9 x 4 = 36
10.	7 x 8 = 56	28.	12 x 12 = 144
11.	5 x 12 = 60	29.	12 x 9 = 108
12.	5 x 4 = 20	30.	8 x 2 = 16
13.	6 x 7 = 42	31.	7 x 10 = 70
14.	11 x 12 = 121	32.	3 x 8 = 24
15.	6 x 4 = 24	33.	8 x 10 = 80
16.	12 x 6 = 72	34.	4 x 4 = 16
17.	7 x 9 = 63	35.	3 x 7 = 21
18.	8 x 8 = 64	36.	9 x 9 = 81

20   Total Problems: ___ Total Correct: ___ Score: ___

© Carson-Dellosa CD-2212

Page 21

Name _____   Using Grouping Symbols

Find the missing factor and write it on the line provided.

1. __8__ x 4 = 32   5. __4__ x 4 = 16   9. 7 x __4__ = 28

2. 7 x __5__ = 35   6. __4__ x 6 = 24   10. __5__ x 5 = 25

3. __4__ x 9 = 36   7. __9__ x 8 = 72   11. 8 x __7__ = 56

4. __7__ x 7 = 49   8. 9 x __6__ = 54   12. 3 x __9__ = 27

Solve to find the unknown amount. Work inside the parentheses first. Pay attention to the operation signs. Write the answer on the line provided.

13. (5 x 2) x 3 = __30__   17. (3 x 3) + (8 x 2) = __25__

14. (7 x 4) x __2__ = 56   18. (3 x 4) + (7 x 7) = __61__

15. (3 + 8) x 9 = __99__   19. (2 x 7) – (3 x 1) = __11__

16. (4 x 4) + (__5__ x 2) = 26   20. (9 x 5) – 15 = __30__

© Carson-Dellosa CD-2212

Total Problems: Total Correct: Score: **21**

Page 22

Name _____   Two- and Three-Digit Multiplication

Multiply. Then, write the answer in the space provided.

1. 66 x 10 = 660   5. 215 x 28 = 6,020   9. 428 x 27 = 11,556   13. 75 x 19 = 1,425

2. 28 x 12 = 336   6. 309 x 19 = 5,871   10. 257 x 66 = 16,962   14. 410 x 67 = 27,470

3. 43 x 16 = 688   7. 455 x 76 = 34,580   11. 989 x 49 = 48,461   15. 636 x 73 = 46,428

4. 746 x 85 = 63,410   8. 758 x 93 = 70,494   12. 849 x 79 = 67,071   16. 964 x 83 = 80,012

22   Total Problems: Total Correct: Score:

© Carson-Dellosa CD-2212

Page 23

Name _____   Two- and Three-Digit Multiplication

Multiply. Then, write the answer in the space provided.

1. 246 x 10 = 2,460   5. 752 x 60 = 45,120   9. 551 x 47 = 25,897   13. 221 x 24 = 5,304

2. 545 x 20 = 10,900   6. 958 x 64 = 61,312   10. 367 x 58 = 21,286   14. 119 x 68 = 8,092

3. 316 x 30 = 9,480   7. 862 x 37 = 31,894   11. 255 x 84 = 21,420   15. 401 x 97 = 38,897

4. 814 x 40 = 32,560   8. 377 x 42 = 15,834   12. 799 x 79 = 63,121   16. 655 x 18 = 11,790

© Carson-Dellosa CD-2212

Total Problems: Total Correct: Score: **23**

Page 24

Name _____   Multiplication Practice

Multiply. Then, write the answer in the space provided.

1. 44 x 2 = 88   5. 114 x 28 = 3,192   9. 306 x 247 = 75,582   13. 226 x 505 = 114,130

2. 75 x 18 = 1,350   6. 684 x 20 = 13,680   10. 528 x 458 = 241,824   14. 456 x 618 = 281,808

3. 86 x 37 = 3,182   7. 897 x 33 = 29,601   11. 654 x 856 = 559,824   15. 575 x 731 = 420,325

4. 94 x 36 = 3,384   8. 832 x 45 = 37,440   12. 740 x 160 = 118,400   16. 911 x 399 = 363,489

24   Total Problems: Total Correct: Score:

© Carson-Dellosa CD-2212

© Carson-Dellosa CD-2212

Multiplication Estimation

Name _____

Round each number to its highest place value. Mulitply. Then, write the answer in the space provided.

1.
$$
\begin{array}{r} 32 \\ \times 11 \end{array}
$$
$$
\begin{array}{r} 30 \\ \times 10 \\ \hline 300 \end{array}
$$

2.
$$
\begin{array}{r} 64 \\ \times 24 \end{array}
$$
$$
\begin{array}{r} 60 \\ \times 20 \\ \hline 1,200 \end{array}
$$

3.
$$
\begin{array}{r} 81 \\ \times 65 \end{array}
$$
$$
\begin{array}{r} 80 \\ \times 70 \\ \hline 5,600 \end{array}
$$

4.
$$
\begin{array}{r} 97 \\ \times 31 \end{array}
$$
$$
\begin{array}{r} 100 \\ \times 30 \\ \hline 3,000 \end{array}
$$

5.
$$
\begin{array}{r} 233 \\ \times 49 \end{array}
$$
$$
\begin{array}{r} 200 \\ \times 50 \\ \hline 10,000 \end{array}
$$

6.
$$
\begin{array}{r} 546 \\ \times 40 \end{array}
$$
$$
\begin{array}{r} 500 \\ \times 40 \\ \hline 20,000 \end{array}
$$

7.
$$
\begin{array}{r} 859 \\ \times 67 \end{array}
$$
$$
\begin{array}{r} 900 \\ \times 70 \\ \hline 63,000 \end{array}
$$

8.
$$
\begin{array}{r} 747 \\ \times 36 \end{array}
$$
$$
\begin{array}{r} 700 \\ \times 40 \\ \hline 28,000 \end{array}
$$

9.
$$
\begin{array}{r} 3,251 \\ \times 267 \end{array}
$$
$$
\begin{array}{r} 3,000 \\ \times 300 \\ \hline 900,000 \end{array}
$$

10.
$$
\begin{array}{r} 6,589 \\ \times 785 \end{array}
$$
$$
\begin{array}{r} 7,000 \\ \times 800 \\ \hline 5,600,000 \end{array}
$$

11.
$$
\begin{array}{r} 5,642 \\ \times 222 \end{array}
$$
$$
\begin{array}{r} 6,000 \\ \times 200 \\ \hline 1,200,000 \end{array}
$$

12.
$$
\begin{array}{r} 9,738 \\ \times 554 \end{array}
$$
$$
\begin{array}{r} 10,000 \\ \times 600 \\ \hline 6,000,000 \end{array}
$$

13.
$$
\begin{array}{r} 8,759 \\ \times 202 \end{array}
$$
$$
\begin{array}{r} 9,000 \\ \times 200 \\ \hline 1,800,000 \end{array}
$$

14.
$$
\begin{array}{r} 11,528 \\ \times 243 \end{array}
$$
$$
\begin{array}{r} 12,000 \\ \times 200 \\ \hline 2,400,000 \end{array}
$$

15.
$$
\begin{array}{r} 9,095 \\ \times 186 \end{array}
$$
$$
\begin{array}{r} 9,000 \\ \times 200 \\ \hline 1,800,000 \end{array}
$$

16.
$$
\begin{array}{r} 26,305 \\ \times 1,172 \end{array}
$$
$$
\begin{array}{r} 30,000 \\ \times 1,000 \\ \hline 30,000,000 \end{array}
$$

Total Problems: _____ Total Correct: _____ Score: _____ **25**

Multiplication Practice

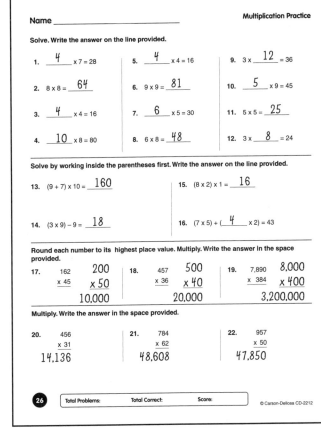

Name _____

Solve. Write the answer on the line provided.

1. __4__ x 7 = 28
2. 8 x 8 = __64__
3. __4__ x 4 = 16
4. __10__ x 8 = 80
5. __4__ x 4 = 16
6. 9 x 9 = __81__
7. __6__ x 5 = 30
8. 6 x 8 = __48__
9. 3 x __12__ = 36
10. __5__ x 9 = 45
11. 5 x 5 = __25__
12. 3 x __8__ = 24

Solve by working inside the parentheses first. Write the answer on the line provided.

13. (9 + 7) x 10 = __160__
14. (3 x 9) – 9 = __18__
15. (8 x 2) x 1 = __16__
16. (7 x 5) + (__4__ x 2) = 43

Round each number to its highest place value. Multiply. Write the answer in the space provided.

17.
$$
\begin{array}{r} 162 \\ \times 45 \end{array}
$$
$$
\begin{array}{r} 200 \\ \times 50 \\ \hline 10,000 \end{array}
$$

18.
$$
\begin{array}{r} 457 \\ \times 36 \end{array}
$$
$$
\begin{array}{r} 500 \\ \times 40 \\ \hline 20,000 \end{array}
$$

19.
$$
\begin{array}{r} 7,890 \\ \times 384 \end{array}
$$
$$
\begin{array}{r} 8,000 \\ \times 400 \\ \hline 3,200,000 \end{array}
$$

Multiply. Write the answer in the space provided.

20.
$$
\begin{array}{r} 456 \\ \times 31 \\ \hline 14,136 \end{array}
$$

21.
$$
\begin{array}{r} 784 \\ \times 62 \\ \hline 48,608 \end{array}
$$

22.
$$
\begin{array}{r} 957 \\ \times 50 \\ \hline 47,850 \end{array}
$$

26 Total Problems: _____ Total Correct: _____ Score: _____

Problem Solving with Multiplication

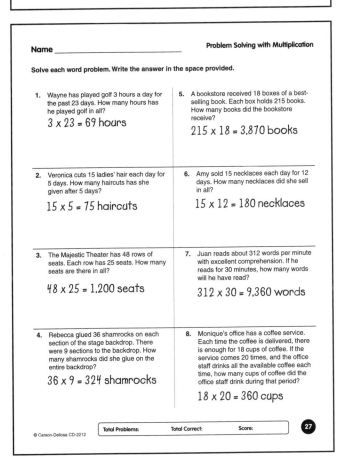

Name _____

Solve each word problem. Write the answer in the space provided.

1. Wayne has played golf 3 hours a day for the past 23 days. How many hours has he played golf in all?

   3 x 23 = 69 hours

2. Veronica cuts 15 ladies' hair each day for 5 days. How many haircuts has she given after 5 days?

   15 x 5 = 75 haircuts

3. The Majestic Theater has 48 rows of seats. Each row has 25 seats. How many seats are there in all?

   48 x 25 = 1,200 seats

4. Rebecca glued 36 shamrocks on each section of the stage backdrop. There were 9 sections to the backdrop. How many shamrocks did she glue on the entire backdrop?

   36 x 9 = 324 shamrocks

5. A bookstore received 18 boxes of a best-selling book. Each box holds 215 books. How many books did the bookstore receive?

   215 x 18 = 3,870 books

6. Amy sold 15 necklaces each day for 12 days. How many necklaces did she sell in all?

   15 x 12 = 180 necklaces

7. Juan reads about 312 words per minute with excellent comprehension. If he reads for 30 minutes, how many words will he have read?

   312 x 30 = 9,360 words

8. Monique's office has a coffee service. Each time the coffee is delivered, there is enough for 18 cups of coffee. If the service comes 20 times, and the office staff drinks all the available coffee each time, how many cups of coffee did the office staff drink during that period?

   18 x 20 = 360 cups

Total Problems: _____ Total Correct: _____ Score: _____ **27**

Basic Division Facts

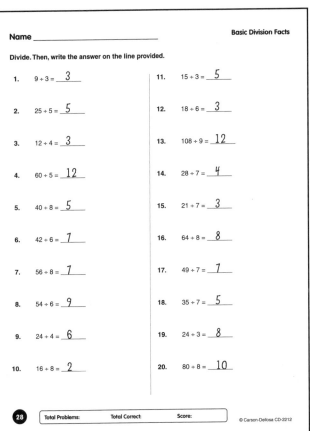

Name _____

Divide. Then, write the answer on the line provided.

1. 9 ÷ 3 = __3__
2. 25 ÷ 5 = __5__
3. 12 ÷ 4 = __3__
4. 60 ÷ 5 = __12__
5. 40 ÷ 8 = __5__
6. 42 ÷ 6 = __7__
7. 56 ÷ 8 = __7__
8. 54 ÷ 6 = __9__
9. 24 ÷ 4 = __6__
10. 16 ÷ 8 = __2__
11. 15 ÷ 3 = __5__
12. 18 ÷ 6 = __3__
13. 108 ÷ 9 = __12__
14. 28 ÷ 7 = __4__
15. 21 ÷ 7 = __3__
16. 64 ÷ 8 = __8__
17. 49 ÷ 7 = __7__
18. 35 ÷ 7 = __5__
19. 24 ÷ 3 = __8__
20. 80 ÷ 8 = __10__

28 Total Problems: _____ Total Correct: _____ Score: _____

Using Grouping Symbols

Name _____

Solve the following number sentences. Always work inside the parentheses first. Then, write the answer on the line provided.

1. (84 ÷ 7) + (9 ÷ 3) = __15__
2. (14 ÷ 2) − (15 ÷ 3) = __2__
3. (12 ÷ 4) + 1 = __3__
4. (18 ÷ 2) + (16 ÷ 8) = __11__
5. (10 ÷ 5) + __11__ = 13

6. (20 ÷ 2) − (10 ÷ 5) = __8__
7. (50 ÷ 5) − (10 ÷ 2) = __5__
8. (36 ÷ 12) + (15 ÷ 3) = __8__
9. (25 ÷ 5) − (14 ÷ 7) = __3__
10. (108 ÷ 12) + (18 ÷ 2) = __18__

Solve the following number sentences, where △ = 5. Write the answer on the line provided.

11. (△ + 5) ÷ 10 = __1__
12. (15 + △) ÷ (8 ÷ 2) = __7__
13. (24 ÷ 3) − △ = __3__
14. (90 ÷ △) + (16 ÷ 8) = __20__
15. (85 ÷ 5) + △ = __22__

16. (100 ÷ 25) + △ + 7 = __16__
17. (60 ÷ △) ÷ 6 = __2__
18. (30 ÷ △) ÷ __2__ = 3
19. (70 ÷ △) + (9 ÷ 3) = __17__
20. (26 − 13) − △ = __8__

© Carson-Dellosa CD-2212

| Total Problems: | Total Correct: | Score: | **29** |

Three- and Four-Digit Dividends

Name _____

Study the rule below. Divide. Then, write the answer in the space provided.

Rule:
Division is the opposite operation of multiplication.

1. 2)264 → 132
6. 3)126 → 42
11. 3)2,466 → 822
16. 6)3,612 → 602

2. 8)648 → 81
7. 5)165 → 33
12. 8)3,288 → 411
17. 8)6,424 → 803

3. 5)700 → 140
8. 7)847 → 121
13. 9)4,545 → 505
18. 9)8,199 → 911

4. 6)240 → 40
9. 4)408 → 102
14. 7)4,914 → 702
19. 7)2,814 → 402

5. 9)729 → 81
10. 6)426 → 71
15. 5)1,805 → 361
20. 4)2,600 → 650

30

| Total Problems: | Total Correct: | Score: |

© Carson-Dellosa CD-2212

Division Practice

Name _____

Divide. Then, write the answer in the space provided.

1. 5)875 → 175
5. 8)3,551 → 443 R7
9. 6)3,612 → 602
13. 15)9,045 → 603

2. 3)7,982 → 2,660 R2
6. 4)7,668 → 1,917
10. 12)426 → 35 R6
14. 8)32,865 → 4,108

3. 6)240 → 40
7. 9)7,548 → 838 R6
11. 10)6,780 → 678
15. 16)32,847 → 2,052 R15

4. 7)5,014 → 716 R2
8. 5)1,025 → 205
12. 8)19,577 → 2,447 R1
16. 5)75,020 → 15,004

© Carson-Dellosa CD-2212

| Total Problems: | Total Correct: | Score: | **31** |

Estimating Quotients

Name _____

Study the rule below. Round the dividend to its highest place value. Divide. Then, write the answer in the space provided.

Rule:
When estimating solutions to division problems, round the number in the dividend, then divide to get the estimated quotient.

1. 5)320 → 5)300 → 60
5. 4)7,776 → 4)8,000 → 2,000
9. 10)6,980 → 10)7,000 → 700

2. 3)882 → 3)900 → 300
6. 9)8,562 → 9)9,000 → 1,000
10. 10)1,160 → 10)1,000 → 100

3. 4)299 → 4)300 → 75
7. 5)2,436 → 5)2,000 → 400
11. 8)4,781 → 8)5,000 → 625

4. 6)5,559 → 6)6,000 → 1,000
8. 2)4,224 → 2)4,000 → 2,000
12. 4)7,890 → 4)8,000 → 2,000

32

| Total Problems: | Total Correct: | Score: |

© Carson-Dellosa CD-2212

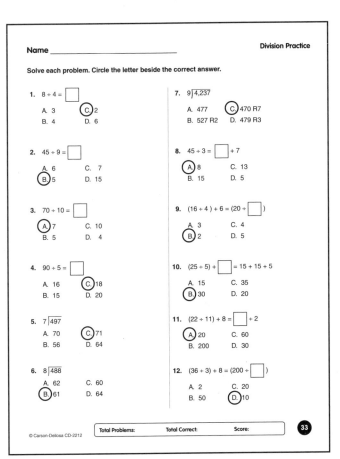

Name _____ Division Practice

Solve each problem. Circle the letter beside the correct answer.

1. $8 \div 4 = \square$
   A. 3   C. 2 ⃝
   B. 4   D. 6

2. $45 \div 9 = \square$
   A. 6   C. 7
   B. 5 ⃝   D. 15

3. $70 \div 10 = \square$
   A. 7 ⃝   C. 10
   B. 5   D. 4

4. $90 \div 5 = \square$
   A. 16   C. 18 ⃝
   B. 15   D. 20

5. $7\overline{)497}$
   A. 70   C. 71 ⃝
   B. 56   D. 64

6. $8\overline{)488}$
   A. 62   C. 60
   B. 61 ⃝   D. 64

7. $9\overline{)4,237}$
   A. 477   C. 470 R7 ⃝
   B. 527 R2   D. 479 R3

8. $45 \div 3 = \square + 7$
   A. 8 ⃝   C. 13
   B. 15   D. 5

9. $(16 \div 4) + 6 = (20 \div \square)$
   A. 3   C. 4
   B. 2 ⃝   D. 5

10. $(25 \div 5) + \square = 15 + 15 + 5$
    A. 15   C. 35
    B. 30 ⃝   D. 20

11. $(22 \div 11) + 8 = \square \div 2$
    A. 20 ⃝   C. 60
    B. 200   D. 30

12. $(36 \div 3) + 8 = (200 \div \square)$
    A. 2   C. 20
    B. 50   D. 10 ⃝

| Total Problems: | Total Correct: | Score: |

© Carson-Dellosa CD-2212   **33**

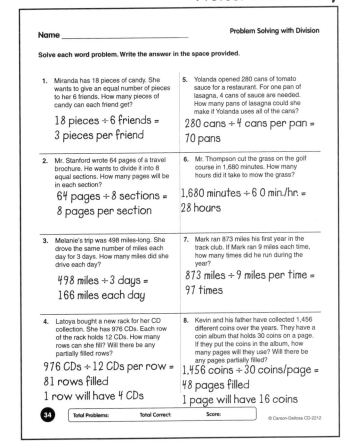

Name _____ Problem Solving with Division

Solve each word problem. Write the answer in the space provided.

1. Miranda has 18 pieces of candy. She wants to give an equal number of pieces to her 6 friends. How many pieces of candy can each friend get?

   18 pieces ÷ 6 friends = 3 pieces per friend

2. Mr. Stanford wrote 64 pages of a travel brochure. He wants to divide it into 8 equal sections. How many pages will be in each section?

   64 pages ÷ 8 sections = 8 pages per section

3. Melanie's trip was 498 miles-long. She drove the same number of miles each day for 3 days. How many miles did she drive each day?

   498 miles ÷ 3 days = 166 miles each day

4. Latoya bought a new rack for her CD collection. She has 976 CDs. Each row of the rack holds 12 CDs. How many rows can she fill? Will there be any partially filled rows?

   976 CDs ÷ 12 CDs per row = 81 rows filled
   1 row will have 4 CDs

5. Yolanda opened 280 cans of tomato sauce for a restaurant. For one pan of lasagna, 4 cans of sauce are needed. How many pans of lasagna could she make if Yolanda uses all of the cans?

   280 cans ÷ 4 cans per pan = 70 pans

6. Mr. Thompson cut the grass on the golf course in 1,680 minutes. How many hours did it take to mow the grass?

   1,680 minutes ÷ 6 0 min./hr. = 28 hours

7. Mark ran 873 miles his first year in the track club. If Mark ran 9 miles each time, how many times did he run during the year?

   873 miles ÷ 9 miles per time = 97 times

8. Kevin and his father have collected 1,456 different coins over the years. They have a coin album that holds 30 coins on a page. If they put the coins in the album, how many pages will they use? Will there be any pages partially filled?

   1,456 coins ÷ 30 coins/page = 48 pages filled
   1 page will have 16 coins

34 | Total Problems: | Total Correct: | Score: |

© Carson-Dellosa CD-2212

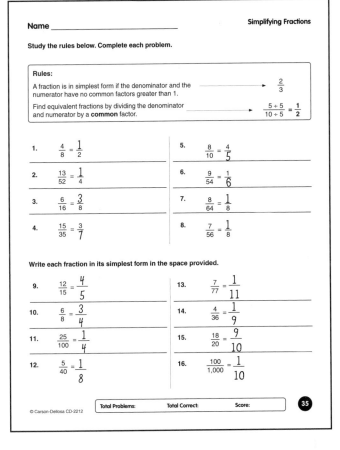

Name _____ Simplifying Fractions

Study the rules below. Complete each problem.

Rules:

A fraction is in simplest form if the denominator and the numerator have no common factors greater than 1. → $\dfrac{2}{3}$

Find equivalent fractions by dividing the denominator and numerator by a **common** factor. → $\dfrac{5 \div 5}{10 \div 5} = \dfrac{1}{2}$

1. $\dfrac{4}{8} = \dfrac{1}{2}$
2. $\dfrac{13}{52} = \dfrac{1}{4}$
3. $\dfrac{6}{16} = \dfrac{3}{8}$
4. $\dfrac{15}{35} = \dfrac{3}{7}$
5. $\dfrac{8}{10} = \dfrac{4}{5}$
6. $\dfrac{9}{54} = \dfrac{1}{6}$
7. $\dfrac{8}{64} = \dfrac{1}{8}$
8. $\dfrac{7}{56} = \dfrac{1}{8}$

Write each fraction in its simplest form in the space provided.

9. $\dfrac{12}{15} = \dfrac{4}{5}$
10. $\dfrac{6}{8} = \dfrac{3}{4}$
11. $\dfrac{25}{100} = \dfrac{1}{4}$
12. $\dfrac{5}{40} = \dfrac{1}{8}$
13. $\dfrac{7}{77} = \dfrac{1}{11}$
14. $\dfrac{4}{36} = \dfrac{1}{9}$
15. $\dfrac{18}{20} = \dfrac{9}{10}$
16. $\dfrac{100}{1,000} = \dfrac{1}{10}$

| Total Problems: | Total Correct: | Score: |

© Carson-Dellosa CD-2212   **35**

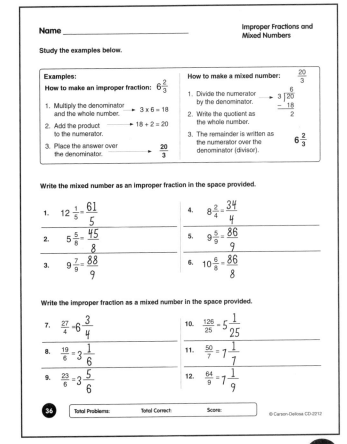

Name _____ Improper Fractions and Mixed Numbers

Study the examples below.

Examples:

How to make an improper fraction: $6\frac{2}{3}$

1. Multiply the denominator and the whole number. → 3 x 6 = 18
2. Add the product to the numerator. → 18 + 2 = 20
3. Place the answer over the denominator. → $\dfrac{20}{3}$

How to make a mixed number: $\dfrac{20}{3}$

1. Divide the numerator by the denominator. → $3\overline{)20}$ $\begin{array}{r} 6 \\ -18 \\ \hline 2 \end{array}$
2. Write the quotient as the whole number.
3. The remainder is written as the numerator over the denominator (divisor). → $6\frac{2}{3}$

Write the mixed number as an improper fraction in the space provided.

1. $12\frac{1}{5} = \dfrac{61}{5}$
2. $5\frac{5}{8} = \dfrac{45}{8}$
3. $9\frac{7}{9} = \dfrac{88}{9}$
4. $8\frac{2}{4} = \dfrac{34}{4}$
5. $9\frac{5}{9} = \dfrac{86}{9}$
6. $10\frac{6}{8} = \dfrac{86}{8}$

Write the improper fraction as a mixed number in the space provided.

7. $\dfrac{27}{4} = 6\frac{3}{4}$
8. $\dfrac{19}{6} = 3\frac{1}{6}$
9. $\dfrac{23}{6} = 3\frac{5}{6}$
10. $\dfrac{126}{25} = 5\frac{1}{25}$
11. $\dfrac{50}{7} = 7\frac{1}{7}$
12. $\dfrac{64}{9} = 7\frac{1}{9}$

36 | Total Problems: | Total Correct: | Score: |

© Carson-Dellosa CD-2212

Least Common Denominator

Name _____

Study the box below. Add or subtract. Write the sum or difference in simplest form in the space provided.

Rule:	Example:
1. Find a common denominator when adding or subtracting fractions with unlike denominators.	$\frac{1}{2} + \frac{1}{10} =$
2. For each fraction, multiply the numerator by the same factor as the denominator.	$\frac{1 (x 5)}{2 (x 5)} = \frac{5}{10}$ $+ \frac{1 (x 1)}{10 (x1)} = \frac{1}{10}$
3. Use the renamed fractions to solve the problem. Reduce if necessary.	$\frac{6}{10} = \frac{3}{5}$

1. $\frac{4}{9} + \frac{1}{3} = \frac{7}{9}$

6. $\frac{8}{9} - \frac{1}{6} = \frac{13}{18}$

2. $\frac{5}{10} + \frac{2}{5} = \frac{9}{10}$

7. $\frac{1}{2} + \frac{2}{3} = 1\frac{1}{6}$

3. $\frac{5}{6} - \frac{3}{18} = \frac{12}{18} = \frac{2}{3}$

8. $\frac{1}{5} + \frac{4}{15} = \frac{7}{15}$

4. $\frac{8}{9} - \frac{2}{3} = \frac{2}{9}$

9. $\frac{7}{8} - \frac{3}{4} = \frac{1}{8}$

5. $\frac{3}{5} - \frac{3}{7} = \frac{6}{35}$

10. $\frac{4}{11} + \frac{2}{3} = 1\frac{1}{33}$

© Carson-Dellosa CD-2212   Total Problems: Total Correct: Score: **37**

Adding and Subtracting Fractions

Name _____

Study the examples below. Find the sum or difference. Remember to find a common denominator before adding or subtracting. Simplify your answer in the space provided.

Examples:

$\frac{3}{8} + \frac{4}{8} = \frac{7}{8}$ ← (3 + 4 = 7)

$\frac{7}{12} - \frac{4}{8} =$ $\frac{7 (x 2)}{12 (x 2)} = \frac{14}{24}$ $- \frac{4 (x 3)}{8 (x 3)} = \frac{12}{24}$ $\frac{2}{24} = \frac{1}{12}$

1. $\frac{2}{3} - \frac{1}{3} = \frac{1}{3}$

2. $\frac{5}{6} - \frac{1}{3} = \frac{1}{2}$

3. $\frac{4}{9} + \frac{1}{3} = \frac{7}{9}$

4. $\frac{5}{10} + \frac{2}{5} = \frac{9}{10}$

5. $\frac{3}{5} + \frac{9}{10} = 1\frac{1}{2}$

6. $\frac{3}{5} + \frac{4}{9} = 1\frac{2}{45}$

7. $\frac{5}{9} - \frac{2}{9} = \frac{1}{3}$

8. $\frac{5}{6} - \frac{3}{18} = \frac{2}{3}$

9. $\frac{3}{7} + \frac{2}{3} = 1\frac{2}{21}$

10. $\frac{5}{6} - \frac{3}{6} = \frac{1}{3}$

11. $\frac{4}{11} + \frac{2}{3} = 1\frac{1}{33}$

12. $\frac{9}{14} - \frac{3}{7} = \frac{3}{14}$

13. $\frac{2}{7} + \frac{5}{14} = \frac{9}{14}$

14. $\frac{2}{3} - \frac{1}{6} = \frac{1}{2}$

15. $\frac{13}{16} - \frac{5}{16} = \frac{1}{2}$

16. $\frac{10}{15} - \frac{2}{10} = \frac{7}{15}$

17. $\frac{3}{4} + \frac{1}{2} = 1\frac{1}{4}$

18. $\frac{2}{3} + \frac{5}{7} = 1\frac{8}{21}$

19. $\frac{2}{3} + \frac{1}{6} = \frac{5}{6}$

20. $\frac{3}{4} - \frac{1}{12} = \frac{1}{12}$...

38   Total Problems: Total Correct: Score: © Carson-Dellosa CD-2212

Subtracting Mixed Numbers

Name _____

Complete each problem. Then, write the answer in the space provided.

1. $6\frac{1}{2} - 1\frac{3}{4} = 4\frac{3}{4}$

2. $15\frac{1}{6} - 11\frac{7}{10} = 3\frac{7}{15}$

3. $9\frac{2}{5} - 8\frac{1}{2} = \frac{9}{10}$

4. $10\frac{1}{3} - 1\frac{2}{3} = 8\frac{2}{3}$

5. $8\frac{3}{10} - 2\frac{7}{10} = 5\frac{3}{5}$

6. $15\frac{2}{3} - 3\frac{3}{4} = 11\frac{11}{12}$

7. $17\frac{3}{6} - 13\frac{5}{6} = 3\frac{2}{3}$

8. $19\frac{1}{2} - 8\frac{2}{3} = 10\frac{5}{6}$

9. $17\frac{2}{3} - 8\frac{1}{9} = 9\frac{5}{9}$

10. $15\frac{1}{2} - 14 = 1\frac{1}{2}$

11. $13\frac{7}{8} - 1\frac{3}{4} = 12\frac{1}{8}$

12. $10\frac{7}{9} - 9\frac{1}{3} = 1\frac{4}{9}$

13. $18\frac{7}{8} - 1\frac{3}{4} = 17\frac{1}{8}$

14. $9 - 8\frac{1}{2} = \frac{1}{2}$

15. $16\frac{3}{10} - 13\frac{5}{6} = 2\frac{7}{15}$

16. $2\frac{1}{10} - 1\frac{1}{6} = \frac{14}{15}$

17. $14\frac{5}{6} - 12\frac{1}{2} = 2\frac{1}{3}$

18. $14\frac{1}{2} - 7 = 7\frac{1}{2}$

19. $16\frac{2}{3} - 3 = 13\frac{2}{3}$

20. $13\frac{1}{3} - 6\frac{1}{2} = 6\frac{5}{6}$

21. $3\frac{2}{5} - 1\frac{1}{5} = 2\frac{1}{5}$

© Carson-Dellosa CD-2212   Total Problems: Total Correct: Score: **39**

Multiplying Fractions

Name _____

Study the box below. Multiply. Write the answer in simplest form in the space provided.

Rule:	Example:
1. Multiply the numerators.	$\frac{1}{3} \times \frac{3}{10} = \frac{3}{30} = \frac{1}{10}$
2. Multiply the denominators.	
3. Write the product in simplest form.	

1. $\frac{2}{3} \times \frac{5}{7} = \frac{10}{21}$

2. $\frac{4}{7} \times \frac{2}{9} = \frac{8}{63}$

3. $\frac{3}{8} \times \frac{3}{4} = \frac{9}{32}$

4. $\frac{5}{6} \times \frac{2}{5} = \frac{1}{3}$

5. $\frac{2}{4} \times \frac{1}{2} = \frac{1}{4}$

6. $\frac{5}{9} \times \frac{1}{5} = \frac{1}{9}$

7. $\frac{1}{2} \times \frac{4}{9} = \frac{2}{9}$

8. $\frac{2}{3} \times \frac{3}{10} = \frac{1}{5}$

9. $\frac{1}{3} \times \frac{5}{6} = \frac{5}{18}$

10. $\frac{1}{8} \times \frac{1}{10} = \frac{1}{80}$

11. $\frac{2}{7} \times \frac{1}{3} = \frac{2}{21}$

12. $\frac{4}{5} \times \frac{7}{8} = \frac{7}{10}$

13. $\frac{2}{7} \times \frac{5}{9} = \frac{10}{63}$

14. $\frac{2}{3} \times \frac{3}{5} = \frac{2}{15}$

15. $\frac{7}{9} \times \frac{1}{2} = \frac{7}{18}$

40   Total Problems: Total Correct: Score: © Carson-Dellosa CD-2212

Name _____ Multiplying Mixed Numbers

Study the example below. Multiply. Write each product in simplest form in the space provided.

Rule:	Example:
To multiply mixed numbers:	$5\frac{1}{4} \times \frac{2}{3} =$
1. Make the mixed number an improper fraction. Multiply the two fractions.	$\frac{21}{4} \times \frac{2}{3} = \frac{42}{12}$
2. Simplify the answer.	$\frac{42}{12} = 3\frac{6}{12} = \mathbf{3\frac{1}{2}}$

1. $1\frac{1}{3} \times \frac{2}{3} = \frac{8}{9}$

2. $8\frac{2}{5} \times 3\frac{1}{8} = 26\frac{1}{4}$

3. $4\frac{1}{2} \times \frac{2}{3} = 3$

4. $\frac{2}{5} \times 5\frac{1}{2} = 2\frac{1}{5}$

5. $\frac{1}{2} \times 6\frac{2}{3} = 3\frac{1}{3}$

6. $2\frac{1}{2} \times 2\frac{1}{3} = 3\frac{5}{6}$

7. $6 \times 3\frac{3}{4} = 22\frac{1}{2}$

8. $8\frac{2}{5} \times \frac{1}{2} = 4\frac{1}{5}$

9. $1\frac{1}{6} \times 4\frac{3}{4} = 5\frac{13}{14}$

10. $2\frac{1}{4} \times 3\frac{2}{3} = 8\frac{1}{4}$

11. $\frac{3}{8} \times 4\frac{2}{3} = 1\frac{3}{4}$

12. $12\frac{1}{5} \times 4\frac{2}{15} = 50\frac{32}{75}$

Total Problems: ___ Total Correct: ___ Score: ___ **41**

© Carson-Dellosa CD-2212

Name _____ Problem Solving with Fractions

Solve each word problem. Write the answers in the space provided.

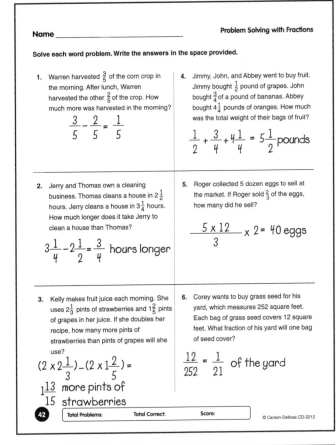

1. Warren harvested $\frac{3}{5}$ of the corn crop in the morning. After lunch, Warren harvested the other $\frac{2}{5}$ of the crop. How much more was harvested in the morning?

$$\frac{3}{5} - \frac{2}{5} = \frac{1}{5}$$

2. Jerry and Thomas own a cleaning business. Thomas cleans a house in $2\frac{1}{2}$ hours. Jerry cleans a house in $3\frac{1}{4}$ hours. How much longer does it take Jerry to clean a house than Thomas?

$$3\frac{1}{4} - 2\frac{1}{2} = \frac{3}{4} \text{ hours longer}$$

3. Kelly makes fruit juice each morning. She uses $2\frac{1}{3}$ pints of strawberries and $1\frac{2}{5}$ pints of grapes in her juice. If she doubles her recipe, how many more pints of strawberries than pints of grapes will she use?

$$(2 \times 2\frac{1}{3}) - (2 \times 1\frac{2}{5}) =$$
$$1\frac{13}{15} \text{ more pints of strawberries}$$

4. Jimmy, John, and Abbey went to buy fruit. Jimmy bought $\frac{1}{2}$ pound of grapes. John bought $\frac{3}{4}$ of a pound of bananas. Abbey bought $4\frac{1}{4}$ pounds of oranges. How much was the total weight of their bags of fruit?

$$\frac{1}{2} + \frac{3}{4} + 4\frac{1}{4} = 5\frac{1}{2} \text{ pounds}$$

5. Roger collected 5 dozen eggs to sell at the market. If Roger sold $\frac{2}{3}$ of the eggs, how many did he sell?

$$\frac{5 \times 12}{3} \times 2 = 40 \text{ eggs}$$

6. Corey wants to buy grass seed for his yard, which measures 252 square feet. Each bag of grass seed covers 12 square feet. What fraction of his yard will one bag of seed cover?

$$\frac{12}{252} = \frac{1}{21} \text{ of the yard}$$

42 Total Problems: ___ Total Correct: ___ Score: ___

© Carson-Dellosa CD-2212

Name _____ Place Value

Study the rule below. Write each number as a decimal in the space provided.

Rule:

tens	ones	.	tenths	hundredths	thousandths
8	7	.	5	4	9

The decimal point separates the whole number from the parts of the whole.
Read this number as: **eighty-seven and five hundred forty-nine-thousandths**
Write this number as a decimal: **87.549**

1. six and twenty-three-thousandths
   6.023
2. four and seventy-six-hundredths
   4.76
3. four hundred thirty-thousandths
   .430

4. fifty-three-thousandths
   .053
5. fifty-three-hundredths
   .53
6. twenty-nine and five-thousandths
   29.005

Write the words for each decimal in the space provided.

7. 6.789 six and seven hundred eighty-nine-thousandths

8. 0.293 two hundred ninety-three-thousandths

9. 2,929.874 two thousand nine hundred twenty-nine and eight hundred seventy-four-thousandths

10. 9.768 nine and seven hundred sixty-eight-thousandths

11. 0.600 six-tenths or six hundred-thousandths

12. 0.003 three-thousandths

13. 4.510 four and five hundred ten-thousandths

14. 2,000.02 two thousand and two-hundredths

Write the value of the underlined digit on the line provided.

15. 0.007 thousandths
16. 2.087 hundredths
17. 75.854 tenths
18. 127.90 ones

19. 3,897.003 thousandths
20. 12.738 hundredths
21. 437.04 hundredths
22. 3,543.21 thousands

Total Problems: ___ Total Correct: ___ Score: ___ **43**

© Carson-Dellosa CD-2212

Name _____ Addition and Subtraction with Decimals

Study the examples below. Add or subtract. Line up the decimal points when you rewrite the problem vertically. Write the answer in the space provided.

Examples:	$53.89 + 50.37 =$	$43.89 - 22.78 =$
	Rewrite the addition problem vertically.	Rewrite the subtraction problem vertically.
	1 1	
	53.89 Line up the decimal points.	43.89 Line up the decimal points.
	+ 50.37 Add each place value and	− 22.78 Subtract each place value
	104.26 carry as needed.	**21.11** and borrow as needed.

1. $10.10 + 3.56 = 13.66$

2. $7.79 - 5.34 = 2.45$

3. $567.009 - 65.87 = 501.139$

4. $654.90 + 87.09 = 74.99$

5. $48.23 + 93.9 = 142.13$

6. $87.09 - 9.02 = 78.07$

7. $60.87 - 23.1 = 37.77$

8. $12.322 + 1.003 = 13.325$

9. $19.3 - 8 = 11.3$

10. $942.35 + 1.233 = 943.583$

11. $400 - .98 = 399.02$

12. $34.1 + .413 = 34.513$

13. $67.9 - 7.9 = 60$

14. $14.87 + .09 = 14.96$

15. $9.76 + 7.99 = 17.75$

16. $56.9 + 8.9 + 6.3 = 72.1$

17. $876.09 - 45.8 = 830.29$

18. $5.8 + 9.7 + 5.1 = 20.6$

19. $700 - .98 = 699.02$

20. $2.349 + 482.2 = 484.549$

21. $0.87 - 0.54 = .33$

44 Total Problems: ___ Total Correct: ___ Score: ___

© Carson-Dellosa CD-2212

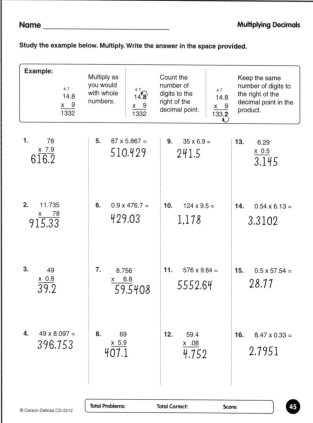

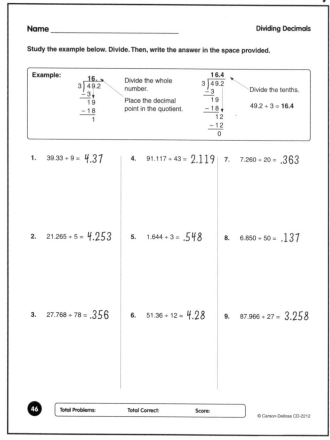

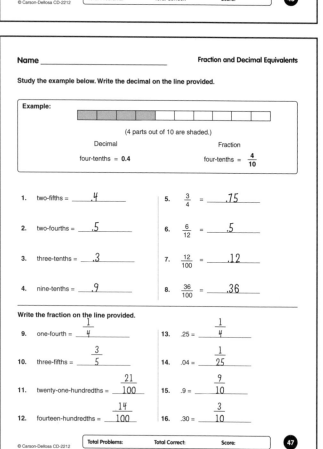

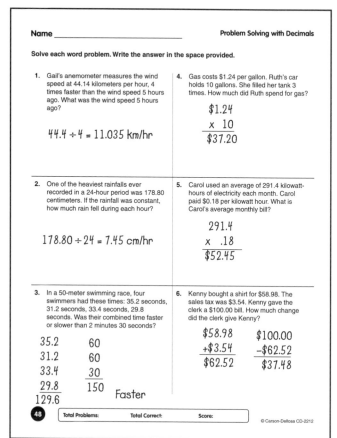

Worksheet 49 — Writing and Comparing Ratios

Name _____ Writing and Comparing Ratios

Study the box below. Write each ratio three different ways in the space provided.

Rule:	Example:
A **ratio** compares two quantities.	7 bananas to 9 monkeys $\frac{7}{9}$ 7 : 9 7 to 9 This ratio can be written three ways.

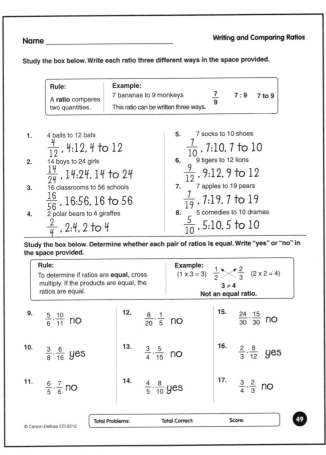

1. 4 balls to 12 bats
$\frac{4}{12}$, 4:12, 4 to 12

2. 14 boys to 24 girls
$\frac{14}{24}$, 14:24, 14 to 24

3. 16 classrooms to 56 schools
$\frac{16}{56}$, 16:56, 16 to 56

4. 2 polar bears to 4 giraffes
$\frac{2}{4}$, 2:4, 2 to 4

5. 7 socks to 10 shoes
$\frac{7}{10}$, 7:10, 7 to 10

6. 9 tigers to 12 lions
$\frac{9}{12}$, 9:12, 9 to 12

7. 7 apples to 19 pears
$\frac{7}{19}$, 7:19, 7 to 19

8. 5 comedies to 10 dramas
$\frac{5}{10}$, 5:10, 5 to 10

Study the box below. Determine whether each pair of ratios is equal. Write "yes" or "no" in the space provided.

Rule:	Example:
To determine if ratios are **equal**, cross multiply. If the products are equal, the ratios are equal.	(1 x 3 = 3) $\frac{1}{2}$ ⤫ $\frac{2}{3}$ (2 x 2 = 4) 3 ≠ 4 **Not an equal ratio.**

9. $\frac{5}{6}, \frac{10}{11}$ no

10. $\frac{3}{8}, \frac{6}{16}$ yes

11. $\frac{6}{5}, \frac{7}{6}$ no

12. $\frac{8}{20}, \frac{1}{5}$ no

13. $\frac{3}{4}, \frac{5}{15}$ no

14. $\frac{4}{5}, \frac{8}{10}$ yes

15. $\frac{24}{30}, \frac{15}{30}$ no

16. $\frac{2}{3}, \frac{8}{12}$ yes

17. $\frac{3}{4}, \frac{2}{3}$ no

© Carson-Dellosa CD-2212   Total Problems: ___ Total Correct: ___ Score: ___   **49**

Worksheet 50 — Understanding Percents

Name _____ Understanding Percents

Study the box below. Write each percent as a fraction. Simplify each fraction. Then, write the answer in the space provided.

Rule:	Example:
A percent is a ratio that compares a quantity to 100.	85 correct questions to 100 total questions $85\% = \frac{85}{100} = \frac{17}{20}$

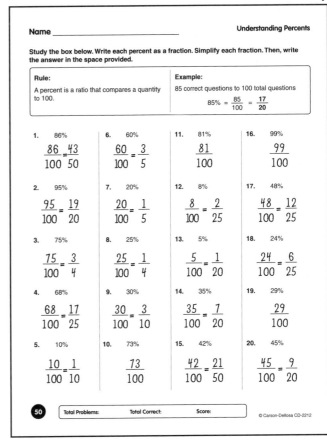

1. 86% $\frac{86}{100} = \frac{43}{50}$

2. 95% $\frac{95}{100} = \frac{19}{20}$

3. 75% $\frac{75}{100} = \frac{3}{4}$

4. 68% $\frac{68}{100} = \frac{17}{25}$

5. 10% $\frac{10}{100} = \frac{1}{10}$

6. 60% $\frac{60}{100} = \frac{3}{5}$

7. 20% $\frac{20}{100} = \frac{1}{5}$

8. 25% $\frac{25}{100} = \frac{1}{4}$

9. 30% $\frac{30}{100} = \frac{3}{10}$

10. 73% $\frac{73}{100}$

11. 81% $\frac{81}{100}$

12. 8% $\frac{8}{100} = \frac{2}{25}$

13. 5% $\frac{5}{100} = \frac{1}{20}$

14. 35% $\frac{35}{100} = \frac{7}{20}$

15. 42% $\frac{42}{100} = \frac{21}{50}$

16. 99% $\frac{99}{100}$

17. 48% $\frac{48}{100} = \frac{12}{25}$

18. 24% $\frac{24}{100} = \frac{6}{25}$

19. 29% $\frac{29}{100}$

20. 45% $\frac{45}{100} = \frac{9}{20}$

50 Total Problems: ___ Total Correct: ___ Score: ___   © Carson-Dellosa CD-2212

Worksheet 51 — Percent of a Number

Name _____ Percent of a Number

Study the examples below. Find the percent for each number using one of the two methods. Then, write the answer in the space provided.

Examples:	Method One: using fractions	Method Two: using decimals
$75\% = \frac{75}{100} = \frac{3}{4}$	75% of 60 $\frac{3}{4} \times 60$ equals **45**	75% of 60 .75 x 60 equals **45**

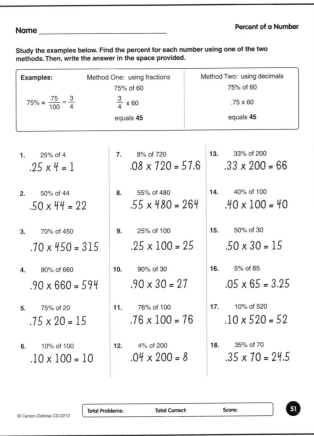

1. 25% of 4
.25 x 4 = 1

2. 50% of 44
.50 x 44 = 22

3. 70% of 450
.70 x 450 = 315

4. 90% of 660
.90 x 660 = 594

5. 75% of 20
.75 x 20 = 15

6. 10% of 100
.10 x 100 = 10

7. 8% of 720
.08 x 720 = 57.6

8. 55% of 480
.55 x 480 = 264

9. 25% of 100
.25 x 100 = 25

10. 90% of 30
.90 x 30 = 27

11. 76% of 100
.76 x 100 = 76

12. 4% of 200
.04 x 200 = 8

13. 33% of 200
.33 x 200 = 66

14. 40% of 100
.40 x 100 = 40

15. 50% of 30
.50 x 30 = 15

16. 5% of 65
.05 x 65 = 3.25

17. 10% of 520
.10 x 520 = 52

18. 35% of 70
.35 x 70 = 24.5

© Carson-Dellosa CD-2212   Total Problems: ___ Total Correct: ___ Score: ___   **51**

Worksheet 52 — Ratio and Percent Practice

Name _____ Ratio and Percent Practice

Solve each problem. Circle the letter beside the correct answer.

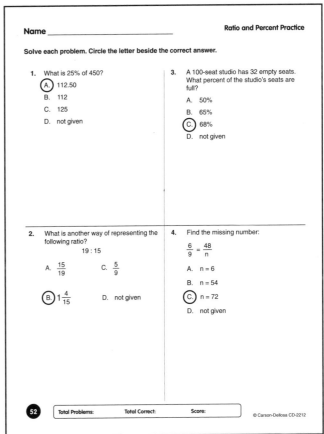

1. What is 25% of 450?
   A. 112.50 (circled)
   B. 112
   C. 125
   D. not given

2. What is another way of representing the following ratio?
   19 : 15
   A. $\frac{15}{19}$ C. $\frac{5}{9}$
   B. $1\frac{4}{15}$ (circled)   D. not given

3. A 100-seat studio has 32 empty seats. What percent of the studio's seats are full?
   A. 50%
   B. 65%
   C. 68% (circled)
   D. not given

4. Find the missing number:
   $\frac{6}{9} = \frac{48}{n}$
   A. n = 6
   B. n = 54
   C. n = 72 (circled)
   D. not given

52 Total Problems: ___ Total Correct: ___ Score: ___   © Carson-Dellosa CD-2212

Name _____   Problem Solving with Ratio
and Percents

Solve each word problem. Write the answer in the space provided.

1. Pia's class planned a hiking trip during spring break. Only 30% of Pia's class went on the trip. If there were 60 people in her class, how many people went hiking?

.30 x 60 = 18 people

3. A total of 541 passengers bought tickets from Fly-Away Airways in four days. If 143 flew on the first and third days and 255 flew on the fourth day, how many flew on the second day?

143
143
+255
541

2. Fred has $250.00 to spend for his summer vacation. He budgeted 20% of his money for souvenirs. How much money did he budget for souvenirs?

$250 x .2 = $50

4. Travis is driving from Kansas City to Dallas on business. He drives at a rate of 95 miles every 2 hours. How far would he drive in 3 hours?

.95 ÷ 2 = 47.5

47.5
x 3
142.5 miles

| Total Problems: | Total Correct: | Score: |

© Carson-Dellosa CD-2212

53

Name _____   Elapsed Time

Find each time. All times for problems 1 through 6 are P.M. Write the answer on the line provided.

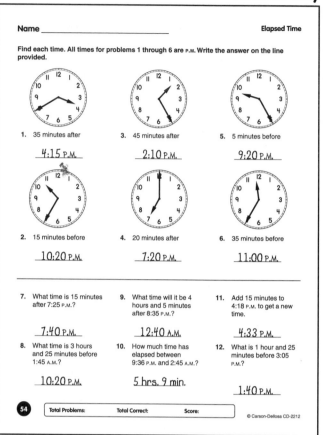

1. 35 minutes after
4:15 P.M.

3. 45 minutes after
2:10 P.M.

5. 5 minutes before
9:20 P.M.

2. 15 minutes before
10:20 P.M.

4. 20 minutes after
7:20 P.M.

6. 35 minutes before
11:00 P.M.

7. What time is 15 minutes after 7:25 P.M.?
7:40 P.M.

9. What time will it be 4 hours and 5 minutes after 8:35 P.M.?
12:40 A.M.

11. Add 15 minutes to 4:18 P.M. to get a new time.
4:33 P.M.

8. What time is 3 hours and 25 minutes before 1:45 A.M.?
10:20 P.M.

10. How much time has elapsed between 9:36 P.M. and 2:45 A.M.?
5 hrs. 9 min.

12. What is 1 hour and 25 minutes before 3:05 P.M.?
1:40 P.M.

54

| Total Problems: | Total Correct: | Score: |

© Carson-Dellosa CD-2212

Name _____   Reading a Schedule

Use the schedule to answer the questions. Then, write your answer on the line provided.

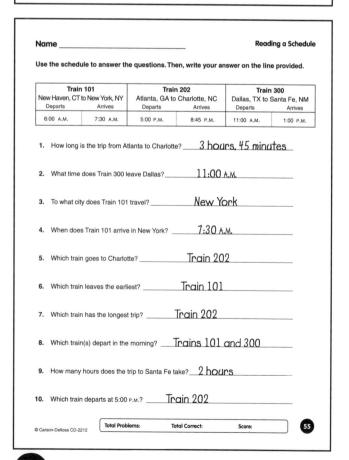

Train 101		Train 202		Train 300	
New Haven, CT to New York, NY		Atlanta, GA to Charlotte, NC		Dallas, TX to Santa Fe, NM	
Departs	Arrives	Departs	Arrives	Departs	Arrives
6:00 A.M.	7:30 A.M.	5:00 P.M.	8:45 P.M.	11:00 A.M.	1:00 P.M.

1. How long is the trip from Atlanta to Charlotte? ____ 3 hours, 45 minutes

2. What time does Train 300 leave Dallas? ____ 11:00 A.M.

3. To what city does Train 101 travel? ____ New York

4. When does Train 101 arrive in New York? ____ 7:30 A.M.

5. Which train goes to Charlotte? ____ Train 202

6. Which train leaves the earliest? ____ Train 101

7. Which train has the longest trip? ____ Train 202

8. Which train(s) depart in the morning? ____ Trains 101 and 300

9. How many hours does the trip to Santa Fe take? ____ 2 hours

10. Which train departs at 5:00 P.M.? ____ Train 202

© Carson-Dellosa CD-2212

| Total Problems: | Total Correct: | Score: |

55

Name _____   Reading Calendars

Use the calendars to answer the questions. Then, write the answer on the line provided.

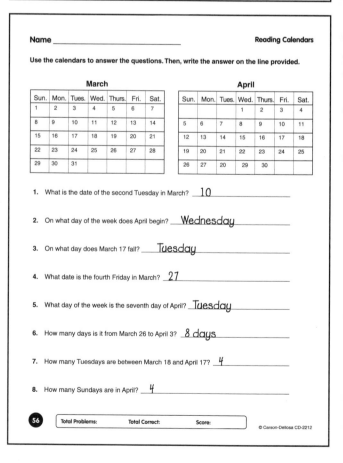

			March			
Sun.	Mon.	Tues.	Wed.	Thurs.	Fri.	Sat.
1	2	3	4	5	6	7
8	9	10	11	12	13	14
15	16	17	18	19	20	21
22	23	24	25	26	27	28
29	30	31				

			April			
Sun.	Mon.	Tues.	Wed.	Thurs.	Fri.	Sat.
			1	2	3	4
5	6	7	8	9	10	11
12	13	14	15	16	17	18
19	20	21	22	23	24	25
26	27	28	29	30		

1. What is the date of the second Tuesday in March? ___ 10

2. On what day of the week does April begin? ___ Wednesday

3. On what day does March 17 fall? ___ Tuesday

4. What date is the fourth Friday in March? ___ 27

5. What day of the week is the seventh day of April? ___ Tuesday

6. How many days is it from March 26 to April 3? ___ 8 days

7. How many Tuesdays are between March 18 and April 17? ___ 4

8. How many Sundays are in April? ___ 4

56

| Total Problems: | Total Correct: | Score: |

© Carson-Dellosa CD-2212

Worksheet 57

Name _____

Problem Solving with Time and Calendars

Solve each word problem. Write the answer in the space provided.

1. Marcus wants to go to work 1 hour and 40 minutes early on Monday. He usually goes to work at 7:30 A.M. What time will he go to work on Monday?

   5:50 A.M.

2. Nathan went to the ball game at 5:45 P.M. He returned to his house 3 hours and 50 minutes after he left. What time did he return?

   9:35 P.M.

3. Melissa wanted to attend her sister's soccer game at 3:30 and see a movie that starts at 4:15. If the game lasts 50 minutes, will she be on time for the movie?

   no

4. Jarron and Kyle rode their bikes for 2 hours and 24 minutes. They left Kyle's house at 4:00 P.M. What time did they return?

   6:24 P.M.

5. Selina went to baby-sit at 5:00 P.M. Saturday night. The parents returned at 9:30 P.M. How long did Selina baby-sit that evening?

   $4\frac{1}{2}$ hours

6. Mr. Miller left his office at 7:15 P.M. He went to the gym for 1 hour and 20 minutes and to the store for another 32 minutes. Then, he went home. What time did Mr. Miller arrive home?

   9:07 P.M.

7. Amy left for her friend's birthday party at 1:20 P.M. It took her mother 24 minutes to drive to the girl's house. What time did Amy arrive at the party?

   1:44 P.M.

8. The Coastal Drink Factory opens for employees at 6:00 A.M. and closes at 11:30 P.M. How many hours is the business open each day?

   $17\frac{1}{2}$ hours

Total Problems: _____ Total Correct: _____ Score: _____ **57**

© Carson-Dellosa CD-2212

Worksheet 58

Name _____

Estimating, Adding, and Subtracting Money

Study the examples below. Estimate. Then, find the actual sums and differences, compare to each estimate, and write the answer in the space provided.

Examples:

Round to the nearest $0.10.	Round to the nearest $1.00.	Round to the nearest $10.00.
$0.85 → $.90	$8.39 → $8.00	$34.60 + $47.30 =
+$0.29 → $.30	+$2.75 → $3.00	$30.00 + $50.00 =
$1.20	**$11.00**	**$80.00**

1. $302.76 + $98.57 = $300 / +$100 / $400   **$401.33**

2. $63.89 − $24.23 $60 / −$20 / $40   **$39.66**

3. $32.51 / $17.25 / +$9.62 $30 / $20 / +$10 / $60   **$59.38**

4. $1,501.69 − $928.72 $1,500 / − $900 / $600   **$572.97**

5. $1.34 + $4.56 = $1.00 / +$5.00 / $6.00   **$5.90**

6. $77.29 − $9.58 = $80 / −$10 / $70   **$67.71**

7. $18.25 / $14.45 / +$6.56 $20 / $10 / +$10 / $40   **$39.26**

8. $45.78 − $26.09 = $50 / − $30 / $20   **$19.69**

9. $49.64 / $26.05 / $9.98 / +$73.02 $50 / $30 / $10 / +$70 / $160   **$158.69**

10. $7.74 − $5.46 $8 / −$6 / $2   **$2.28**

11. $6.59 / $8.25 / +$1.45 $7 / $8 / + $1 / $16   **$16.29**

12. $38.74 / $29.07 / +$56.86 $40 / $30 / +$60 / $130   **$124.67**

58   Total Problems: _____ Total Correct: _____ Score: _____

© Carson-Dellosa CD-2212

Worksheet 59

Name _____

Multiplying and Dividing Money

Study the box below. Complete each problem in the space provided. Be sure to place the numbers in the correct place value and watch the placement of the decimal point.

Rule:

$165.28
+ 163.20
$328.48

If there are 2 numbers to the right of the decimal, there should be 2 numbers to the right of the decimal point in the product.

Example: $3.76

```
    $3.76
 4)15.04
   −12
    3 0
   −2 8
     24
    −24
      0
```

Place the decimal point in the quotient. It goes in the same place as in the dividend.

1. $264.98 x 9 = **$2,384.82**

2. $18.79 x 8 = **$150.32**

3. $113.96 ÷ 4 = **$28.49**

4. $42.36 x 12 = **$508.32**

5. $149.94 ÷ 6 = **$24.99**

6. $92.82 x 21 = **$1,949.22**

7. $124.02 ÷ 9 = **$13.78**

8. $171.24 ÷ 12 = **$14.27**

Total Problems: _____ Total Correct: _____ Score: _____ **59**

© Carson-Dellosa CD-2212

Worksheet 60

Name _____

Problem Solving with Money

Solve each word problem. Then, write the answer in the space provided. Where appropriate, write the dollar sign and the decimal (cent) point in the answer.

1. Jake has $15.00 to spend for a Mother's Day gift. He wants to buy roses. They cost $2.50 each. How many roses can Jake purchase?

   $15 ÷ $2.50 = 6 roses

2. Sharon went shopping for a surprise birthday party. She spent $14.23 on balloons, $29.61 on a gift, and $28.32 for food. How much did she spend in all?

   $14.23 / $29.61 / +$28.32 / **$72.16**

3. Last year, Carla earned $1,023.59 by cutting grass and doing odd jobs for neighbors. This year, she earned $1,562.22. How much more did Carla earn this year?

   $1,562.22 / −$1,023.59 / **$538.63**

4. Sean went to a hockey game. He spent $6.79 on food, $15.27 on a souvenir puck, and $27.68 on the ticket. How much money did he spend all together?

   $15.27 / $27.68 / +$ 6.79 / **$49.74**

5. Kyle earns $42.78 each week for delivering newspapers. He delivered newspapers for 8 weeks. How much money did Kyle earn in 8 weeks?

   $42.78 / x 8 / **$342.24**

6. Kristi wants to buy 3 shirts for $18.99 each. If she has $75.00, how much money will she have left after buying the shirts?

   $18.99 / x 3 / $56.97 $75.00 / −$56.97 / **$18.03**

60   Total Problems: _____ Total Correct: _____ Score: _____

© Carson-Dellosa CD-2212

Customary Length

Name _____

Study the rules below. Write inches, feet, yards, or miles as appropriate on the line provided.

Rules:	Customary Units	
	12 inches (in) = 1 foot (ft)	1,760 yd = 1 mile (mi)
	3 ft = 1 yard (yd)	5,280 ft = 1 mi

1. The width of a doorway may be 49 **inches**.
2. My father's height is about 6 **feet** tall.
3. I jumped 46 **inches** in the standing long jump.
4. Each morning, I run about 5 **miles** for exercise.
5. I threw the softball 20 **feet** to reach home plate.
6. A desk might be 46 **inches** wide.
7. The distance from Atlanta, GA, to Harrisburg, PA, is about 845 **miles**.
8. The height of my stuffed animal is $7\frac{1}{2}$ **inches**.
9. The width of my television is 36 **inches**.

Choose the appropriate unit of measurement. Write inches (in), feet (ft), yards (yd), or miles (mi) on the line provided.

10. length of a football field: **yd**
11. distance to Mars: **mi**
12. distance you throw a ball: **ft**
13. thickness of a textbook: **in**

Complete. Write the answer on the line provided.

14. 18 ft = **216** in
15. 5 ft 3 in = **63** in
16. 440 yd = **4** mi
17. 10,560 ft = **2** mi
18. 36 in = **3** ft
19. 120 in = **10** ft

Total Problems: ___ Total Correct: ___ Score: ___ **61**
© Carson-Dellosa CD-2212

Customary Mass

Name _____

Study the rules below. Write ounces, pounds, or tons as appropriate on the line provided.

Rules:	Customary Units
	16 ounces (oz) = 1 pound (lb)
	2,000 pounds (lb) = 1 ton (t)

1. An elephant may weigh 2 **tons**.
2. A glass of juice may weigh 6 **ounces**.
3. A car weighs about 1 **ton**.
4. A cat weighs about 9 **pounds**.

Choose the appropriate unit of measurement. Write ounces (oz), pounds (lb), or tons (t) on the line provided.

5. the weight of a potato chip: **oz**
6. the weight of a truck: **t**
7. the weight of a pair of shoes: **lb**
8. the weight of a key: **oz**

Complete. Write the answer on the line provided.

9. 224 oz = **14** lb
10. 80 oz = **5** lb
11. 4 lb = **64** oz
12. 2 t = **4,000** lb
13. 16,000 lb = **8** t
14. 5 t = **160,000** oz
15. 8 lb = **128** oz
16. 500 lb = **.25** t
17. 1.5 lb = **24** oz

62 Total Problems: ___ Total Correct: ___ Score: ___
© Carson-Dellosa CD-2212

Customary Capacity

Name _____

Study the rules below. Write cups, pints, quarts, or gallons as appropriate on the line provided.

Rules:	Customary Units	
	2 cups (c) = 1 pint (pt)	4 qt = 1 gallon (gal)
	2 pt = 1 quart (qt)	16 c = 1 gal

Choose the appropriate unit of measurement. Write cups (c), pints (pt), quarts (qt), or gallons (gal) on the line provided.

1. measuring milk for a brownie mix: **c**
2. gasoline needed for a car: **gal**
3. water for a swimming pool: **gal**
4. measuring a barrel's capacity: **gal**
5. a bowl of soup: **c**
6. a milk jug: **gal**

Complete. Write the answer on the line provided.

7. 2 gal = **8** qt
8. 4 pt = **2** qt
9. 6 c = **3** pt
10. 8 qt = **2** gal
11. 3 gal = **12** qt
12. 3 gal + 2 qt = **56** c
13. **4** pt = 2 qt
14. 3 c = **1.5** pt
15. 2 pt = **4** c
16. 5 qt = **10** pt
17. **2** gal = 16 pt
18. 5 gal = **20** qt

© Carson-Dellosa CD-2212 Total Problems: ___ Total Correct: ___ Score: ___ **63**

Metric Length

Name _____

Study the rules below. Choose the appropriate metric unit of measurement. Write millimeters (mm), centimeters (cm), meters (m), or kilometers (km) on the line provided.

Rules:	Metric Units
	10 millimeters (mm) = 1 centimeter (cm)
	100 cm = 1 meter (m)
	1,000 m = 1 kilometer (km)

1. A car travels at 55 **km** per hour.
2. A thumbtack is 4 **mm** long.
3. A man is about 2 **m** tall.
4. A pen is 15 **cm** long.

Choose the appropriate unit of measurement. Write millimeters (mm), centimeters (cm), meters (m), or kilometers (km) on the line provided.

5. the length of a soccer field: **m**
6. the distance to the sun: **km**
7. a day's ride in the car: **km**
8. the length of a straw: **cm**
9. the width of a pencil eraser: **mm**
10. the length of a classroom: **m**
11. the width of a foot: **cm**
12. the distance to run a marathon: **km**

Complete. Write the answer on the line provided.

13. 48 km = **48,000** m
14. 835.7 cm = **8,357** mm
15. 0.01 m = **1** cm
16. 3 km = **3,000** m
17. 93 cm = **.93** m
18. 756 mm = **.756** m
19. 7,007 mm = **700.7** cm
20. 54 km = **5,400,000** cm

64 Total Problems: ___ Total Correct: ___ Score: ___
© Carson-Dellosa CD-2212

92

© Carson-Dellosa CD-2212

Name _____ Metric Mass

Study the rules below. Choose the appropriate unit of measurement. Write grams (g), milligrams (mg), or kilograms (kg) on the line provided.

> **Rules:** Metric Units
> 1,000 milligrams (mg) = 1 gram (g)
> 1,000 g = 1 kilogram (kg)

1. A gold bracelet might weigh 11 __g__ .

3. A vitamin tablet might weigh 100 __mg__ .

2. A quarter might weigh 3 __g__ .

4. An adult might weigh 90 __kg__ .

Choose the appropriate unit of measurement. Write grams (g), milligrams (mg), or kilograms (kg) on the line provided.

5. a nickel: __g__

9. an orange: __g__

6. a bicycle: __kg__

10. a sewing needle: __mg__

7. a new pencil: __g__

11. a kitchen table: __kg__

8. a gold necklace: __g__

12. a paper clip: __mg__

Complete. Write the answer on the line provided.

13. 3,200 g = __3.2__ kg

17. 7 kg = __7,000,000__ mg

14. __8,000__ g = 8 kg

18. 7 kg = __7,000__ g

15. 3,000 mg = __3__ g

19. 14 kg = __14,000__ g

16. 6,000 mg = __.006__ kg

20. 64 g = __64,000__ mg

Total Problems: ____ Total Correct: ____ Score: ____

Name _____ Temperature

Study the rule below. Then, use the chart to complete the questions. Circle the letter beside the correct answer.

> **Rule:**
> To convert Celsius (C°) to Fahrenheit (F°), multiply the Celsius temperature by 1.8 and add 32.
> To convert Fahrenheit (F°) to Celsius (C°), subtract 32 from the Fahrenheit temperature, multiply the difference by 5, then divide the product by 9.

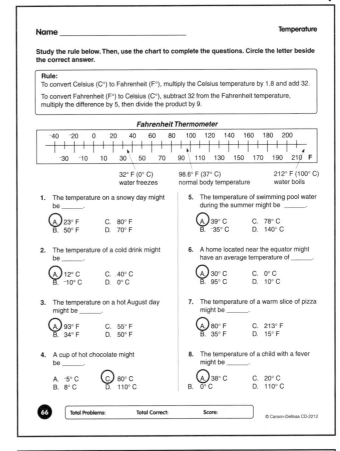

Fahrenheit Thermometer

32° F (0° C) water freezes   98.6° F (37° C) normal body temperature   212° F (100° C) water boils

1. The temperature on a snowy day might be _____.
   A. 23° F C. 80° F
   B. 50° F D. 70° F

5. The temperature of swimming pool water during the summer might be _____.
   A. 39° C C. 78° C
   B. -35° C D. 140° C

2. The temperature of a cold drink might be _____.
   A. 12° C C. 40° C
   B. -10° C D. 0° C

6. A home located near the equator might have an average temperature of _____.
   A. 30° C C. 0° C
   B. 95° C D. 10° C

3. The temperature on a hot August day might be _____.
   A. 93° F C. 55° F
   B. 34° F D. 50° F

7. The temperature of a warm slice of pizza might be _____.
   A. 80° F C. 213° F
   B. 35° F D. 15° F

4. A cup of hot chocolate might be _____.
   A. -5° C C. 80° C
   B. 8° C D. 110° C

8. The temperature of a child with a fever might be _____.
   A. 38° C C. 20° C
   B. 0° C D. 110° C

Total Problems: ____ Total Correct: ____ Score: ____

Name _____ Problem Solving with Measurement

Solve each word problem. Write the answer in the space provided.

1. Gary bakes 10 loaves of bread for the party. He needs 4 cups of milk for each loaf. How many quarts of milk does he need to bake all of the loaves?

   10 quarts

4. Demarcus bought 9 gallons of ice cream for his birthday party. He has 34 guests coming. If each guest eats $2\frac{1}{2}$ cups of ice cream, how many pints of ice cream will be left over?

   29.5 pints

2. Elizabeth needed $1\frac{1}{2}$ gallons of water to water her plants. Her watering can holds 1 quart. How many times will Elizabeth fill her watering can to water her plants?

   6 times

5. Evelyn's swimming pool requires 3 quarts of a bacteria-cleaning agent 5 times a month. How many gallons of this agent will Evelyn use during June, July, and August?

   $11\frac{1}{4}$ **gallons**

3. Matthew delivered 7 containers of orange juice to the Apple Tree Restaurant. Each container had 8 quarts of orange juice. How many gallons of orange juice did Matthew deliver?

   14 gallons

6. Neal changed the oil in his vehicle. The car required 6 quarts of oil. If Neal wants to change his oil every month for a year, how many quarts of oil will Neal need to buy?

   72 quarts

Total Problems: ____ Total Correct: ____ Score: ____

Name _____ Polygons

Study the rules below. Name the polygons. Then, write the answer on the line provided.

Rules:	Vocabulary:	prefix	# of sides
A four-sided figure is called a **quadrilateral**.	A **polygon** is a closed figure that has three or more straight line segments.	penta	5
		hexa	6
	A **closed figure** is a figure that has no open line segments. You can trace a line around the perimeter of a closed figure without ever coming to an end.	hepta	7
		octa	8
		nona	9
		deca	10

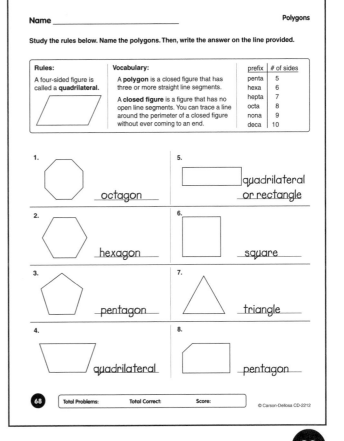

1. __octagon__

5. __quadrilateral or rectangle__

2. __hexagon__

6. __square__

3. __pentagon__

7. __triangle__

4. __quadrilateral__

8. __pentagon__

Total Problems: ____ Total Correct: ____ Score: ____

Worksheet 1 (Angles)

Name _____   Angles

Study the rules below. Identify angles as right, acute, obtuse, or straight. Then, write the answer on the line provided.

Rules:

Right Angle	Acute Angle	Obtuse Angle	Straight Angle
A right angle measures exactly 90 degrees.	An acute angle measures less than 90 degrees.	An obtuse angle measures more than 90 degrees but less than 180 degrees.	A straight angle measures exactly 180 degrees.

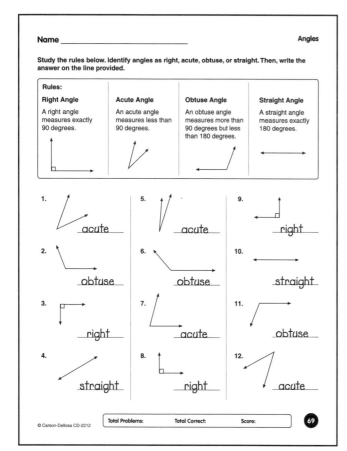

1. acute
2. obtuse
3. right
4. straight
5. acute
6. obtuse
7. acute
8. right
9. right
10. straight
11. obtuse
12. acute

© Carson-Dellosa CD-2212

Total Problems: Total Correct: Score: **69**

Worksheet 2 (Triangles)

Name _____   Triangles

Study the rules below. Write the type of triangle shown on each line provided.

Rules:

Equilateral Triangle	Isoceles Triangle	Scalene Triangle
An equilateral triangle has all three sides of equal length.	At least two sides of an isoceles triangle are of equal length.	Each side of a scalene triangle is a different length.
Right Triangle	**Acute Triangle**	**Obtuse Triangle**
A right triangle has one right angle.	An acute triangle has three acute angles.	An obtuse triangle has one obtuse angle.

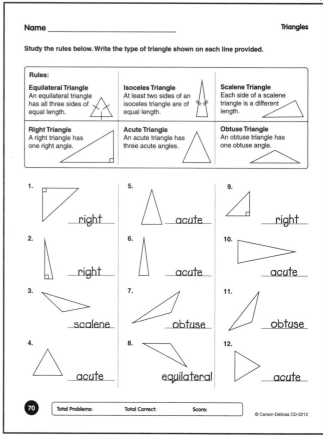

1. right
2. right
3. scalene
4. acute
5. acute
6. acute
7. obtuse
8. equilateral
9. right
10. acute
11. obtuse
12. acute

70   Total Problems: Total Correct: Score: © Carson-Dellosa CD-2212

Worksheet 3 (Circles)

Name _____   Circles

Study the rules below. Write chord, diameter, or radius for the given segment on the line provided.

Rules:

A **chord** is a line segment that has its endpoints on the circle.	A **diameter** is a chord that passes through the center of a circle.	A **radius** is a line segment that has one endpoint on the circle and one endpoint on the center of the circle.

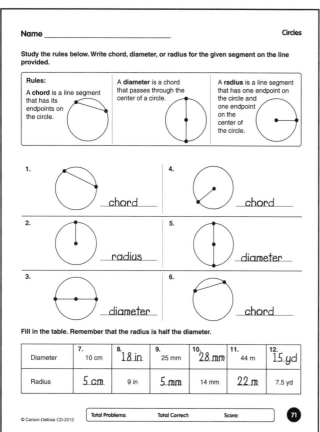

1. chord
2. radius
3. diameter
4. chord
5. diameter
6. chord

Fill in the table. Remember that the radius is half the diameter.

	7.	8.	9.	10.	11.	12.
Diameter	10 cm	18 in	25 mm	28 mm	44 m	15 yd
Radius	5 cm	9 in	5 mm	14 mm	22 m	7.5 yd

© Carson-Dellosa CD-2212

Total Problems: Total Correct: Score: **71**

Worksheet 4 (Perimeter)

Name _____   Perimeter

Study the box below. Find the perimeter of each figure and write it on the line provided.

Rule:
The **perimeter** of a figure is the distance around it. This can be found by adding the measurements of all sides together.

Example:
24 in, 20 in, 20 in, 24 in
24 + 20 + 24 + 20 = **88**
perimeter = 88 inches

1. 10 cm, 7 cm, 7 cm, 5 cm — **29 cm**
2. 11 mm, 11 mm, 4 mm — **26 mm**
3. 7 m, 5 m, 5 m, 7 m — **24 m**
4. 1.5 ft each side — **9 ft**
5. 25 cm, 25 cm — **100 cm**
6. 12 m, 12 m, 24 m, 24 m, 6 m — **78 m**

72   Total Problems: Total Correct: Score: © Carson-Dellosa CD-2212